Work From Home

The Ultimate 6 in 1 Box Set Guide to Making Money With Ebay, Craigslist, Thrift Stores, Garage Sales, Day Trading for Beginners and Amazon Fulfillment!

6 Books in 1

BOX SET

Copyright © 2015

All rights reserved. No part of this book may be reproduced in any form without permission in writing from the author. Reviewers may quote brief passages in reviews.

Disclaimer

No part of this publication may be reproduced or transmitted in any form or by any means, mechanical or electronic, including photocopying or recording, or by any information storage and retrieval system, or transmitted by email without permission in writing from the publisher.

While all attempts and efforts have been made to verify the information held within this publication, neither the author nor the publisher assumes any responsibility for errors, omissions, or opposing interpretations of the content herein.

This book is for entertainment purposes only. The views expressed are those of the author alone, and should not be taken as expert instruction or commands. The reader of this book is responsible for his or her own actions when it comes to reading the book.

Adherence to all applicable laws and regulations, including international, federal, state, and local governing professional licensing, business practices, advertising, and all other aspects of doing business in the US, Canada, or any other jurisdiction is the sole responsibility of the purchaser or reader.

Neither the author nor the publisher assumes any responsibility or liability whatsoever on the behalf of the purchaser or reader of these materials.

Any received slight of any individual or organization is purely unintentional.

Book # 1

eBay

(Includes Bonus Content)

5 Proven Methods for making $1,000+ a Month selling on eBay

Introduction

I want to thank you and congratulate you for downloading the book, "eBay: 5 Proven Methods for making $1,000+ a Month Selling on eBay."

This book contains proven steps and strategies on how you can start making more than $1,000 each month by selling items on eBay.

If you follow the steps that are set forth in this book you will be able to start bringing in an extra income without ever having to work for another person and enjoy the rewards that come from working for yourself on such an easy to use website.

Thanks again for downloading this book, I hope you enjoy it!

Chapter 1: What is eBay?

Most people have big dreams when they are young; thinking of all of the ways that they are going to make a living when they grow up without having to live in the drudgery of the typical workplace. However, the truth is, once you grow up and realize that you have no choice, most people have to make a living doing a whole variety of jobs that they might not enjoy. If this description fits you then you might be looking for a way out of this day to day rut without sacrificing any of the benefits of your current lifestyle. In addition, you probably have thoughts of even improving your lifestyle some.

Selling items on eBay can be just the step for you to take in order to achieve some financial freedom in your life, or even just to add a good source of an extra income to your current earnings. The eBay website was established in 1995 and is one of the best known auctions online all over the world today. In fact, it has gained so much popularity that they registered a whopping 152.3 million users as being active in 2014 already. This means that you can find a huge customer base just waiting for you to sell to them!

With the help of this book, you will not only learn the basics of selling on eBay, you will also learn the 5 proven methods to help you make over $1,000 every month with ease. While eBay is not a free auction website, their fees are reasonable for sellers and you are well protected with every listing you add. This makes it so much easier than attempting to sell things on other venues that might be out there. Let's start off with some of the bare basics of how eBay can make you money.

Chapter 2: How Does eBay Work?

Once you start selling on eBay, you will notice just how simple their whole user interface is and how easily you can get your listings out to the public view. Getting yourself set up on this site is a pretty simple process and it won't take a lot of your time to do, so we will get straight into it.

Setting up Your Account

When you go to the auction website, there is a simple link that says register. All that you have to do from there is fill in your personal information, making sure that it is correct. You will also be linking bank information for payment so make sure that you fill it all in properly and you should definitely make sure that you are verified on PayPal because that's going to be the best way for you to get your payments from your potential customers. All of these verifications help keep you and your buyers nice and secure so that no one ends up being concerned about getting scammed by another.

Add Your Listings

Your next step is to add the items that you want to sell to the eBay site. The first thing to consider is that you need to choose a category that fits the description of your items in a clear manner. This will help your things show up in the searches that shoppers perform and make sure that you get the visibility that you need in order to sell. This is where you will choose your pricing, as well. There are different options for this, including a starting bid, a buy it now price and the cost of shipping. It's important for you to remember that many of the purchases on this website are made by bidding because it is an online auction. This means that some of your listings will go for a higher price than others, just depending on the bids that are placed by other people. You can even set a reserve limit so that if someone bids too low of an amount, you won't have to be worried about selling your item for too little.

Manage Your Business

Make sure that you keep an eye on your items and pay attention to your sales by using the "My Account" option in your seller account on eBay. It's important that you pay attention to what is going on with your sales so that you can address any issues before they turn into a major problem. When you take the first step to making a decent amount of money by selling things on eBay, the first thing to realize is that you always need to treat this like your business. If you go into it with this in mind then you will be more likely to take it seriously and not give up during those little struggles that are inevitable in almost any new venture.

Organize Yourself

Before you add any listings to eBay, you should take a moment to sit down and think about what you want to achieve with your money making venture. Set out a plan based on your profit margin and how much you eventually want to be bringing in every month. If you are intending on making your eBay business your only form of income then you should also pay attention to your household expenses and set up a budget accordingly. It's a good idea to take it slow at first, just to make sure that you get the hang of how to best go about things before you count on it as your sole money maker.

Chapter 3: 5 Methods to Boost Your Income

Now that you understand the basic steps of selling items on eBay, it's time to get even more in depth and start exploring the entire reason that you chose this book. There are people that just sell a few things on this popular auction website and then there are those that come in and conquer the market. Of course, you want to be one of the former, and really learn how to make your time on eBay count by making $1,000 or more every month. Let's look at some ways that you can make this dream your new reality.

Number 1: Know What You Are Selling

If you take away nothing else from this book, this is the most important thing for you to remember. It doesn't matter if you are the best marketer in the world and follow every other method in this book if you are selling the wrong kinds of things. Know your market and know what they like. This means that the very first thing that you need to do is sit down for a little research. Think of some things that you might be interested in selling and see how they are doing on eBay right now. Look at their average pricing and see how high their bids go, not to mention how long it takes for them to sell.

In addition to doing research surrounding your items, make sure that you know enough about your products to effectively sell them to other people with enthusiasm. Being excited about your items will go a long way in convincing others that you are the right person to buy from. After all, there are so many choices online; you have to find a way to make yourself look more appealing than all of those other options. The way to do this is to be knowledgeable and sell with integrity, honesty and by showing these qualities to all of your potential customers.

Number 2: Research, Research, Research

Not only should you do research before you decide what kind of items you would like to start dealing in on eBay, you should not stop just because you have decided on something. In order for you to effectively manage your new business venture and to insure that you are earning the most money that you can every month, you need to stay fluid. Remember that buying trends vary and what might be popular this month can go straight to the back of the line in a couple of months time. Make sure that you continue to watch your selling habits and cater to the changes that become obvious in your inventory.

Number 3: Pay Attention to Timing and Pricing

While it might be tempting to set a high reserve so that you can tempt people to bid without having to lose out on the money that you think that you should actually get for a listing, it's best to shy away from this practice. First of all, many seasoned shoppers on eBay look for reserves and stay well away from them because they can be a hassle on that end. Secondly, you have to pay more fees when you set a reserve on your items so it can be counterproductive to make this your standard practice. That isn't to say that you won't ever use this feature, but it should definitely be few and far between. For the most part when you use eBay, you will want to set a lower starting bid without giving your items away for free and then just let the bidding rise from there. You have the potential to make a lot on many of your listings simply because of the bidding process used by shoppers.

This is also where we should mention a few words on the timing of your listing. You can set your auctions to run for several different amounts of times, but you want to consider these carefully. Don't leave your listing up for too long because that causes people to lose interest in your items and see if they can find them from someone else in a lot less time. Weekends are the most high traffic periods for online shoppers, so your best bet is to list your items for 10 days so that you can hit 2 sets of these shoppers. This also gives your listings enough time to become popular without sitting for so long that everyone forgets about you.

Number 4: Make Your Pictures Count

The only way that potential customers on eBay know what they are buying is if you include a picture of your items with every listing. The first thing to consider about these pictures is to make sure that they are good enough quality to make someone actually want the item that you are selling. You don't have to have a professional photographer on staff, but you should make sure that your images are well lit and that you clearly show the item.

The amount of pictures that you put on your listing is also a huge boost for your sales, so don't skimp! Buyers are much more likely to bid on an item that has several well taken photographs that show each and every facet of the item that you are trying to clear off of your shelves. Make sure that you show the good and bad sides, as well; don't leave little blemishes out of the picture because you always want to be upfront with your customers.

Number 5: Your Description Tells Shoppers Everything

Next to the images that you choose to represent the items that you have listed for sale on eBay, you should also consider the importance of the description that you add to it. This is where you really get the chance to let your products shine, so don't hold back. Make sure that you offer your potential shoppers a detailed description so that they know exactly what they are getting. People are spending their hard earned money, so they want to know that they are spending it in the right place and they want to feel comfortable bidding with you.

Not only should you made the description of the items that you have listed on eBay very detailed, you should also become familiar with search optimization. This doesn't mean you have to do anything special really; it just means that you should think like a customer. When you search for things online you usually know exactly what you are looking for and therefore, those are the words that you type in. It's very important that you include the right kind of search words into your description so that shoppers can find you easily; after all, if no one sees your listing then you can't sell to them.

These are 5 proven methods that will help you earn even more money when you start selling things on the eBay auction website.

Even if you only adhere to this group of tips, you will find yourself bringing in more cash than you ever thought that you could. However, there are a few more things for you to consider so that you can make sure that your journey is smooth and that you reach your top earning potential as quickly as possible. Don't get left behind, keep reading!

Chapter 4: A Few Other Things to Remember

In the previous chapters you learned how to set up your new business on eBay and just how easy it can be. You also learned the 5 proven methods to make your listings stand out from all of the others and start making more than $1,000 each month with only a little bit of effort on your part. Let's explore a few other guidelines for you to follow in order to ensure your success even further and get you on the path to making that cash.

Customer Service is Key

Make sure that you treat each encounter online with the same level of professionalism that you would expect for yourself if you were in the buyer's place instead. Be courteous and use your customer skills to remain friendly even during a return because all of your customers can leave you feedback and you want to make sure that you keep your ratings high so that you come up as a trusted seller. This will make people more likely to want to shop with you because they know that they can trust your items and your shipping habits.

Always Tell the Truth

In addition to showing off your stellar customer service skills, you should always represent your items with honest descriptions.

Never hide things about the items that you list and always make sure that you offer a full disclosure of any flaws or issues, no matter how minor they seem. Even if it seems like you are describing blemishes that no one will notice, it's best to protect yourself from unhappy customers by offering all of the information up front. This also helps give you a good reputation among the shoppers on eBay because they know that you will be truthful about the items that they buy from you.

Obey the Regulations

No matter what, you should always make sure that you read and follow the rules and regulations set forth by eBay. Otherwise, you might have your selling privileges revoked. You can even end up losing any ability to be on eBay at all! This is certainly not something that you want to happen while you are trying to follow your dreams and start making money on this popular website. It isn't difficult to follow their rules so just make sure that you know what they are so that you don't end up crashing your money making abilities before you really get started.

Pay Attention to Spelling and Grammar

When you are writing your description, make sure that you write it in a professional and proper way. If you are using the brand name of the item then make sure that you spell it correctly. Not only will this help you appear like you know what you are talking about, it will also make it easier for your listings to come up in buyers' searches. If you spell the name wrong then you can end up slipping right under their noses. When you are exchanging messages with buyers or potential customers, you should also ensure that you are typing in a legible manner and that you are leaving no room for any misinterpretations by any of the parties involved. This is to help protect you from any disputes as well as help you continue to provide your customers with a pleasant shopping experience.

Ship Purchases with Care

When you have made a sale and it is time to get the items to their new owners you should take care with your packaging and shipping. Label your shipments correctly, verifying the shipping address before you send it off. Pack the items carefully in bubble wrap or other protective materials to ensure that they arrive safely and in the condition that was promised when you listed them. You should also be careful to ship the items that have been purchased within the time that you specified that you would in order to keep your customers happy, returning and spreading your name in a favorable manner.

Leave Feedback

Feedback is the king of eBay, so don't ignore it, even when you are the seller. It can help other people on the website just as much as their feedback can help you, so make sure that you don't neglect leaving good feedback for your good customers. Even if they are a first time shopper with you they will still appreciate getting this from you and that can go a long way in creating a favorable relationship with more customers.

Keep Records of Everything

One more thing that will help take you even farther towards your goals of making more than $1,000 every month by selling on eBay is to learn to keep records. If you run out of stock on your most popular item then you will find yourself frustrated and losing money that could have easily been in your bank account. Keep track of your inventory and pay attention to your best sellers and to the items that just don't seem to be moving well so that you can act accordingly. It's also a good idea to keep track of your sales so that you can see how much you're earning and know if you need to adjust your pricing strategy at all.

These are just a few more ways to help boost your sales when you are selling things on eBay. While many of these tips might seem pretty straightforward, it will benefit you greatly to add them to your use of the 5 proven methods listed previously in order to maximize your earning potential and make yourself a huge success by using eBay as your online marketplace of choice.

Chapter 5: Putting it All Together

You should now have a clear understanding of what you will need to do so that you can easily earn more than $1,000 each month by selling your items on the eBay website. Everything that you need is listed here for your convenience, from setting up your account and planning out your financials to the best ways to ensure your monetary success.

Just remember to make yourself a plan to follow so that you get everything lined out properly and make sure that you keep decent records of your inventory and your sales in order to keep yourself making money long after the first excitement wears off. Good customer service will take you a long way on your path to making a good income on eBay every month and honesty in your listings will keep people coming back to you when they are shopping online. If you follow the helpful methods laid out in this book and pay attention to the little details then you can be the next top earner with your items on this fantastic auction website. Just remember to stay determined and don't give up on your dreams to add extra earnings to your portfolio and you can be a success with eBay in no time at all.

Chapter 1: Printers

Item # 1:

HP Laser Jet 3050

Max Bid: $25.00

Estimated Selling Range: $80 -$140

Selling Speed: Fast!

Item # 2:

Brother HL- 2280

Max Bid: $15.00

Estimated Selling Range: $50-$80+

Selling Speed: Medium - Fast

Item # 3:

Samsung Xpress

Max Bid: $15.00

Estimated Selling Range: $40-$80

Selling Speed: Fast!

Chapter 2: Athletic Shoes

Item # 4:

La Sportiva

Max Bid: $10.00

Estimated Selling Range: $30-$60+

Selling Speed: Fast!

Item # 5:

Asics Nimbus Running Shoes

Max Bid: $8.00

Estimated Selling Range: $25-$60+

Selling Speed: Medium

Item # 6:

Salomon Techamphibians

Max Bid: $12.00

Estimated Selling Range: $45-$65+

Selling Speed- Medium

Chapter 3: Men's Scarves

Item # 7:

Hermes

Max Bid: $40.00

Estimated Selling Range: $60 - $100+

Selling Speed: Fast!

Item # 8:

Burberry

Max Bid: $10.00

Estimated Selling Range: $30 - $80+

Selling Speed- Fast!

Item # 9:

John Varvatos

Max Bid: $8.00

Estimated Selling Range: $30 - $50+

Selling Speed – Medium

Chapter 4: Bicycles

Item # 10:

Trek Mountain Bicycles

Max Bid: $40.00

Estimated Selling Range: $100-$300+

Selling Speed – Fast

Item # 11:

Cannondale Road Bicycles

Max Bid: $100.00

Estimated Selling Range: $150-$450+

Selling Speed – Fast!

Item # 12:

Rocky Mountain Bicycles

Max Bid: $50 - $100.00

Estimated Selling Range: $125-$350+

Selling Speed- Fast

Chapter 5: Board games

Item # 13:

Hero Quest

Max Bid: $25.00

Estimated Selling Range: $50-$100+

Selling Speed- Fast

Item # 14:

Fireball Island

Max Bid: $50.00

Estimated Selling Range: $150 - $200+

Selling Speed- Fast!

Item # 15:

Dark Tower

Max Bid: $35.00

Estimated Selling Range: $60-$150+

Selling Speed- Medium – Fast

Chapter 6: Backpacks

Item # 16:

Mountain Hardwear

Max Bid: $10

Estimated Selling Range: $30-$60+

Selling Speed- Medium

Item # 17:

Osprey

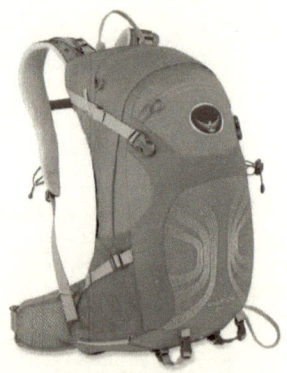

Max Bid: $25.00

Estimated Selling Range: $50-$80+

Selling Speed – Fast!

Bonus Chapter: 10 Tips for making more money on eBay!

Tip # 1: *Source Thrift Stores on Sale Days*

If you want to maximize your profits while selling on eBay one of the best things you can do for your business is to acquire cheap inventory on sale days. If you are not sure whether or not your local thrift stores offer sale days, simple give them a call, and ask. Personally, where I live, my local thrift stores run half off days once a week, every Sunday. With the cost of shipping, eBay fees, supplies, PayPal and so on it is imperative you spend as little money possible when acquiring your inventory to resell.

Tip # 2: *Take Better Pictures*

Taking better pictures may be easier said than done, but to be honest, it's really not that hard to take excellent pictures. I won't go into too much detail here, but to be brief, all you need is a decent camera, a clean backdrop, proper lighting, and some basic editing software, and you are all set to take professional pictures. EBay even offers a free editing tool to clean up all your pictures.

Tip # 3: *Add More Detail to Your eBay Listings*

Adding the necessary details in your listing for a potential customer is huge! I have noticed that many sellers are very vague with their descriptions and don't go above and beyond in terms of item specifics. I think this is a huge mistake and takes a lot of sales away from the seller. Make sure to include the condition, size, measurements, any flaws, color, where item was produced, special selling points, or anything you feel the buyer may want to know to make a purchase right then and there.

Tip #4: *Run Sales in Your Store*

Running sales in your eBay store is huge because it will allow you to make more sales. Making more sales not only will make you more money, but it will shoot a signal to eBay's algorithm letting them know you are a good seller, and that buyers should see your items for sale. Also when running sales I have noticed my eBay listing rank higher in the search engine which is turn puts more eyes on my listings. As you know, the more traffic you get the more sales you will land!

Tip # 5: *Improve Return Policy*

Having a favorable return policy that makes your potential customers on eBay comfortable will work wonders for your business. Many sellers will put "No returns" in their listings and I find that this really throws up a red flag to buyers. If you are running a legitimate business on eBay and have faith in your products, then I feel you should take a leap of faith and accept returns. Of course, some people will take advantage of your return policy, using the item a few times, and then returning it, but in general, I have noticed most people are good people and won't take advantage of you. Plus if a buyer really wants a return all they have to do is start a claim with eBay and put forth " item not described" and they will get their money back anyways. Accept returns, trust me, it will help you make more money in the long run!

Tip # 6: *Include a Thank You Letter*

When I say a thank you letter I don't mean you have to actually write a letter, however, if you feel that motivated to do so then feel free! In all seriousness, all you have to do is include a little thank you card, sticker, or anything that let's your buyer know you appreciate their business. If you go onto eBay and type into the search bar "eBay thank you sticker" you will find the product I use to show my buyers appreciation. This will help you make your customers a lot happier, you will receive more positive feedback, and all in all, you will land more sales and make more money down the road!

Tip # 7: *Offer the Best Customer Service You Can*

Customer service is one of the major traits that will separate the winners from the losers in business. Look at some of the most success businesses in your local area. You will notice they go above and beyond for their customers to make them happy. Remember all it takes is one bad experience for one of your buyers to set off a chain reaction bad mouthing towards your business. Keep your customers happy and you will be much more successful in your eBay business!

Tip # 8: *Ship Fast*

In today's day of age people want to get the items they ordered super fast. Honestly, it's never fast enough! If you offer any more than 1 day shipping and handling time you are losing sales. You may think I am crazy to say that, but honestly, people are in a rush and want their stuff now! Offer 1 day shipping.

Tip # 9: *Give Your Customers Free Shipping*

Offering free shipping for your items for sale on eBay will not only intrigue buyer's to purchase from you, but it will also rank your listings higher in the search engine. On top of that, it will help you to become a top rated seller. There are tons of benefits to offering free shipping. You need to be doing this!

Tip # 10: *Create A Listing Schedule and Follow Through*

Now that you have your business in line and you are ready to be making a lot of money on a consistent basis, now you have to create a listing schedule. The only way you will make money from the items you find at thrift stores, garage sales, and flea markets is to actually list them on eBay. You won't believe how many people miss this step! It's crazy! In order to create a listing schedule take a look at the opening in time you have free to list and make a commitment. I list everyday for at least 2-3 hours. Listings consistently will help you to make a lot more money!

Conclusion

Thank you again for downloading this book!

I hope this book was able to help you to reach your goals to make $1,000+ a moth by selling items on eBay.

The next step is to suggest this book to your friends and relatives, if you feel it will benefit them too. This book can help you realize your full earning potential on this easy to use auction website and give you that extra money in your account every month.

Finally, if you enjoyed this book, please take the time to share your thoughts and post a review on Amazon. It'd be greatly appreciated!

Thank you and good luck!

Book #2

Craigslist

How to Make $2,000+ Every Month Working from Home Part- Time on Craigslist

Introduction

I want to thank you and congratulate you for downloading the book, "Craigslist: How to make $2,000+ Every Month Working from Home Part- Time on Craigslist."

This book contains proven steps and strategies on how to make upwards to $2,000+ a month by working from home on craigslist.

Many people underestimate the importance of

In this book you are going to learn

Thanks again for downloading this book, I hope you enjoy it!

Chapter 1 - How I Made Over $25, 000 My First Year on Craigslist

I had just lost my job in December and my savings account was slowly dwindling down. I was at the point where I had no other choice but to get a job at a fast food joint - just to put food on the table for my family. I was at one of my lowest points in my life and felt helpless. While all seemed to be going wrong and my financial situation *kept getting worse and worse* **something happened**.

Late one night I was watching some YouTube videos from a group of guys who were making money online selling various types of items. One guy was selling on eBay, another was selling on Amazon, and the third fellow was making a full – time income selling items on craigslist.

I'm not exactly sure what happened at that point but a light switched on in my head. I decided I was going to start a craigslist business. The main reason I decided to go this route was because it seemed like the path of least resistance. While eBay and Amazon is known to be great, it is more difficult to get started, and there are a lot more rules one must follow to comply with the selling platform. I didn't have much time to waste and I needed to start making money fast!

January 3rd 2012 I started my Craigslist business with $25 dollars in my pocket and $197 dollars in my bank account. Approximately one year later I had almost $9,000 in savings and had earned over $25,000 in income through my craigslist business.

Now I am not here to say this was an easy journey, it took hours and hours of hard work, I made plenty of mistakes, and I had to consistently push myself to get up in the morning and "Hustle "to make my money on craigslist. That's the thing about running your own business. No one is telling you what to do. It's all about you - the individual; you make your own schedule, you source your own inventory, you list your own products, and you arrange to sell your inventory to potential customers.

At times the process can see intricate in nature and overly complicated. But at the end of the day it takes time. It takes time to learn the business, to figure out what to buy, how to put systems in place that save time and how to get the most out of your craigslist business.

With that being said; I firmly believe if I was able to make $25,000 on craigslist with very little start up cost and with my back against the wall then you could too. I am not the smartest guy in the world or the savviest businessman. I am just a normal guy, an average Joe, a person who did what it took to make enough money to support my family.

Hopefully this has been able to inspire you. I want to teach you all I know and give the exact recipe I followed to succeed on craigslist. Take my hand and let me teach you what I know. It's not that complicated at all!

Chapter 2- Where to Source Profitable Inventory to Sell on Craigslist

Depending on where you live in the country this will play a role in terms of what niche to choose. On top of that, the same applies for how to source quality inventory for your craigslist business. It will be very important that you take a step back, observe what means you have available to source quality inventory, and then hit the ground running!

With that being said, I will go over a few really great ways I source inventory personally, and a few other's I know work, but I don't do myself because of my location. Again everyone is different; some methods of sourcing inventory that work for me won't work for you and vice versa. Take each method with a grain of salt and try them all out to see what's the most effective!

Thrift Stores

Sourcing inventory from thrift stores is probably my favorite way to acquire super awesome inventory that can make me a lot of money on craigslist. Where I live I am literally surrounded by thrift stores that are offering cheap clothing inventory and electronics on a regular basis. Having a large amount of thrift stores in your area can be a great opportunity for you! A quick tip for getting cheap inventory at thrift stores is to go on the half off days. Many thrift stores will dedicate a day to a special discount, or slashed rate, to keep their inventory moving. This is when you need to pounce on the opportunity and get your items dirt cheap!

Yard Sales or Tag Sales

If you live in a pretty populated area; yard sales or otherwise known as tag sales on the east coast is a terrific way to find profitable inventory for your business. I have found Saturday's to be the best day to go to yard sales in terms of finding the best inventory. Make sure if you really want to have a good experience that you plan out a route in advance the night before and you wake up early. As the saying goes, "The early bird get's the worm". This is one of the best methods for acquiring quality inventory on a budget!

Auctions

Personally I rarely ever go to auctions due to the abundance of thrift stores and yard sales I have locally in my general area, but I know of many who love auctions and do very well. In my opinion inventory at auctions will typically be more expensive, and the competition will be higher, but if you have a specialized niche you are very educated in you can do extremely well.

Flea Markets

Flea markets can be very lucrative if you again have specialized knowledge in one or more niche areas. I have a friend who specialized in antiques and makes an absolute killing every weekend! Again, just like the auctions, I rarely use this method due to my area and specialized expertise, but like I said my friend and many other's love this method and you can find some great stuff to resell on craigslist!

Craigslist

Craigslist is probably my 3rd favorite method for acquiring quality inventory to resell on craigslist. Yes I sound buy on craigslist and resell on craigslist – It's possible! Many people underestimate the power of craigslist and don't think that there is anything worth buying on this site besides retail priced items, but I am telling you right now they are dead wrong! When I first got started reselling items, craigslist was the avenue I focused on the most. I like to call this process "sniping"; because I am literally sniping out specific items that are undervalued by sellers.

So now you know the exact methods I used to source my inventory to sell on craigslist. Again like I said, try these out for yourself and see what works for you. We are all different and there is no exact strategy that works best. Test the market; see what yields you the best bang for your buck. Once you figure that out, scale up, and leverage your time – this is the key!

Now let's move onto the next chapter and talk about finding your niche. Determining this will make your life so much easier! Ask yourself this question. *Why run up a hill when you could just run down?* This is what finding a niche can do for you!

Chapter 3- How to Find a money - making Niche in Your Given Location and Get Super Educated

Many people fall under the notion that is it not necessary to have a niche, or bread and butter items you sell often, but from my perspective I think that is a big mistake.

The main reason I think it is smart to formulate a niche, and become an expert on the subject is because it will allow you constantly bring in a steady income. Many times when you become an expert on a certain subject, or type of item, you will have the ability to see and find products that others may look over.

From my own personal experience I specialize in the niche of clothing, bicycles, and antiques. Having this niche allows me to always find a steady flow of inventory even when times seem to be slow in terms of acquiring items to sell on craigslist.

Now in terms of finding a specific niche to focus on, and becoming an expert on it, I would suggest you spend a good amount of time in your local thrift stores, auction houses, yard sales, retail stores, or wherever you go to source your inventory. Reason being is because you will want to determine what type or types of items are plentiful in your geographical area. For me clothing and bicycles is super abundant, cheap, and is found all over the place, for you this may be completely different. In your area you may have an abundance of cheap electronic items, so this may be where you will want to consider focusing your energy. You need to test out your market immediately!

Once you find your niche, and you have determined there is a good opportunity for you to make money off of it on craigslist, now it is time to get educated. The best way to do this is to scan the sold and completed listings on eBay and get comfortable with these types of items. Keep in mind that prices on eBay will be higher than craigslist because it is a bigger market, but just subtract 25% off the top and that's what you should be able to sell the items for.

Study what selling points are causing items to sell, what prices they are selling for, how often they are selling for, etc.

Do this every single day, and before you know it, you will be an expert! This is exactly what I did to discover my niche and become super educated. To be more specific I would spent every night from 8 PM to 10 PM study the sold listings on eBay and scanning through the craigslist categories getting accustomed with what is hot and what is not. There is many strategies you can implement to find a niche and get educated but this is what I used.

Now that you are discovering what niche you should focus on and are becoming educated, next, it's time to start talking about listings your items on craigslist.

Because honestly, you can't make money on the products you source unless you list them.

Listing will make you the money!

Chapter 4- How to List Your Inventory on Craigslist

Step 1: Find Your Local Area

You can search for your given location on the right hand side bar.

Step 2: Choose the Category Which You Will Be Selling Your Item Under

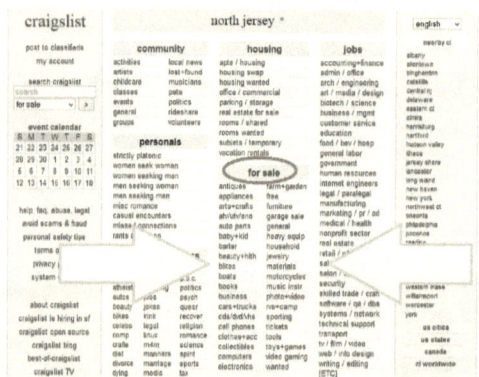

In the next example I chose to sell under the bicycle category. Keep following along!

Step 3: If you are selling as an individual as most of you will be then Choose the "By Owner Tab"

Bicycles:

- ALL BICYCLES
  (dealer + by-owner)
- BY-OWNER ONLY
  (private party, no dealers)
- BY-DEALER ONLY
  (no private party)

Parts & Accessories:

- ALL PARTS & ACCESSORIES
  (dealer + by-owner)
- BY-OWNER ONLY
  (private party, no dealers)
- BY-DEALER ONLY
  (no private party)

Step 4: Hit the Post Tab at the Right Hand Corner of the Page

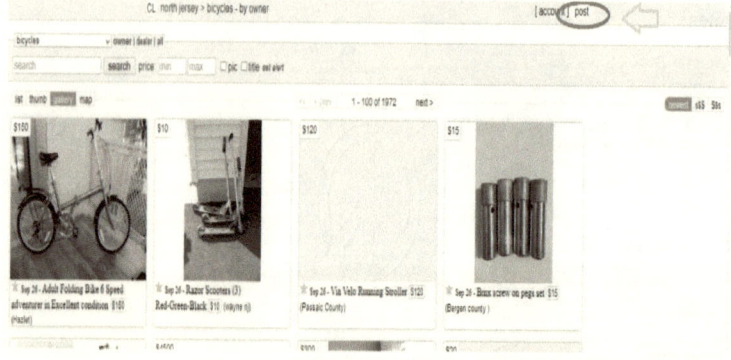

Step 5: Choose What Type of Posting This Is

Note: Again for most of us (99% of people reading this) we will be selling our items "By Owner".

If you are a business or another form of entity you may want to choose differently.

Once this is done **Click Continue.**

Step 6: Confirm the Category One Last Time

Once This Is Done :**Click Continue**

Step 7: Filling out the listing

Now this is the important part. You want to make sure you fill this out as accurately as possible.

Wherever you see the stars in the picture below you will want to be sure to fill out.

Anything unmarked with a star is not necessarily required to fill out.

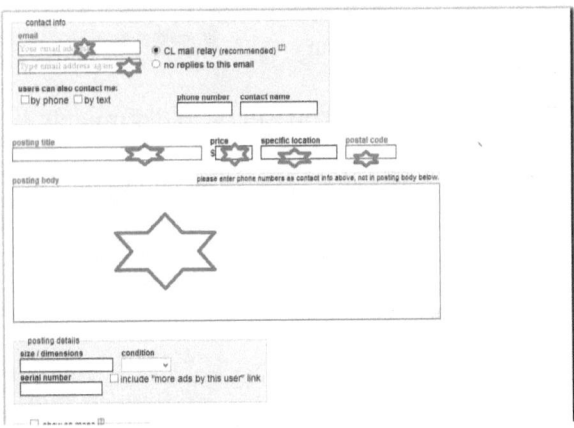

Note: *Make sure you use a valid email address is this will be your primary means of communication with your potential customers.*

Step 8: Add images to your craigslist listing

(Quality images are one of the most important factors in selling your item fast and for a high price. Focus on taking great pictures)

The camera I use is a Canon Power shot. You can the older models used for less than $100 used. This is a great point and shoot camera for craigslist.

Step 9: Publish Your Craigslist Listing

(Note: At this point be sure to double check you're listing for accuracy. Add or remove any information that is or isn't necessary)

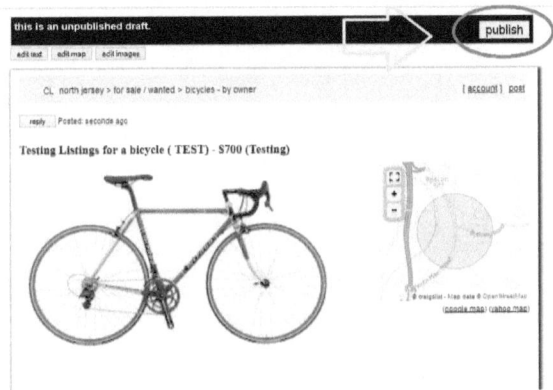

Step 10: Confirm Listing in Email Provided and Accept Terms of Use to Finalize

Part 1

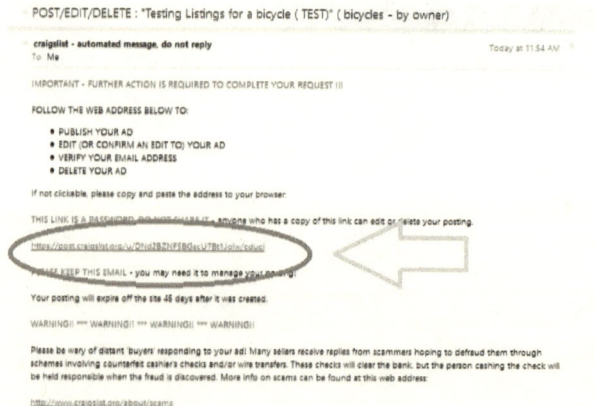

Part 2

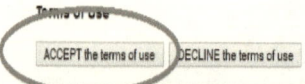

Step 11: View Live Craigslist Post

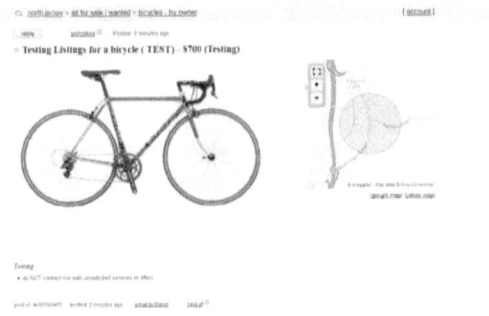

So there you have it. Now that you have been walked through the entire process step by step of listing your items on craigslist you are now ready to learn some safety tips.

Honestly craigslist is a very safe place to sell. But there have been some occasions where people have found themselves in trouble.

You can avoid that easily by following some basic guidelines. See you in the next chapter!

Chapter 5- Safety Tips for Selling on Craigslist

Just like anything in life there are precautions one must take in order to ensure their safety. Craigslist is no different.

Below I will list some tips for staying safe while selling on craigslist to ensure your safety.

All in all I please ask you to just use some common sense. 90% of the time just thinking a little bit will keep you safe.

Tip # 1: *Follow your intuition* – If you have a bad feeling about a potential buyer then don't test the waters. A lot of buyer's will flake out and waste your time. Also some buyer's will try to low ball you the last minute. If you feel like things are adding up –trust your intuition and cancel the meet – up.

Tip # 2: *Don't Meet At Your Home-* Now this is my opinion but in all honestly I don't want my customers knowing where I live. What if something goes wrong? What if the item breaks 6 months down the road? Do you really want them knocking at your door and retaliating. Odds are this won't happen but I prefer to meet up with customers outside of the house.

Tip#3: *Meet in a populated area*- In my opinion this is the best place to sell items to potential customers. Many people who have been robbed or stolen from on craigslist would have avoided that situation if they had met in a populated area. Most people who are planning to rob you want to meet in an isolated location where cameras and other people are not present. If someone is persistent on meeting in a discreet unpopulated area this should be a huge RED FLAG.

Tip # 4: *Never Give Out Personal Information* – When I say personal information never give away your last name, address, social security number, credit card information or anything like this.

Tip # 5: *Only accept Cash*- This is a must! If you want to get burned then accept credit card or checks. NEVER DO THIS. People who are on craigslist to scam people will always try to pay via money orders, checks, or fake credit cards. Don't do it!

Tip # 6: *Never Ship Items*- Again, scammers and thieves will try to get you to ship items. They may send you a check then have you ship the item. Once they receive the item and you go to cash the check it will bounce. Don't do this. Only meet in person for cash!

Tip # 7: *Never Front Items*- Remember in the introduction of this chapter I talked about using your common sense? Well this is a perfect example. Use your head and don't front items. If someone wants an item then they will have to pay cash at the time of the transaction. Don't believe any excuses, justification, or promises sellers make on craigslist. If they don't have cash then pass!

Now that you have read this chapter you are now all ready to safely run a craigslist business. Please do not make exceptions to these rules. If you do, you risk at getting robbed, conned, or ripped off!' Now let's move on and talk about some strategies you can use to sell your items faster and for a higher price than your competition!

Chapter 6- 5 Tips for Selling Your Items Faster and for a Higher Price than Your Competition

Selling your items faster and for a higher price than your competition can be easier said than done at times, but if you follow these tips, you will put yourself in a better position to do so!

Tip # 1: Take Amazing Pictures

A picture is worth a thousand words could have never been more true especially when it comes to selling on craigslist. If you take great pictures, show all the important details, use good light, and avoid too many background distractions your customers will appreciate this! I see so many craigslist pictures of poor quality and this really affects their ability to sell the items quickly and for a good profit.

Tip # 2: Don't overprice your items

Before you price your items make sure to do your due diligence. The worst thing you could do is create a beautiful listing, add a ton of detailed information in the description, and yet fail when it comes to pricing the item. If you price an item too high you will steer away your potential customers. Research first!

Tip # 3: Quickly Respond to Emails and Phone calls and meet up with potential customers in a timely manner

When I had first gotten started with my craigslist business I wasn't meeting up with my potential customers fast enough. A person would contact me about buying a bicycle and I would make them wait 2 or 3 days before I would schedule a date. To be honest I was being lazy, and was only making things work when it was convenient for me. This is the wrong way to go about things. You have to take this business serious and be willing to hustle when the calling appears. When you make people wait they will go elsewhere. I lost a lot of deals because of this. Eventually as time went on I smartened up and made it super easy and convenient for customers to buy my items. This is huge!

Tip #4: Create a detailed and honest listing description so your potential customers can make a buying decision fast!

Make sure when you create your craigslist listing that you put a lot of detail in the description. If you are selling a leather jacket make sure you include the size, color, measurements, item specifics and so on. Also, if there are any flaws make sure to include them and take lots of pictures. Don't get lazy on this portion of the listing. Going above and beyond for your customers at this point will tremendously help you to outshine your competition and make more sales!

Tip #5: Constantly relisting your items when they become outdated.

After a certain period of time your listing will expire on craigslist. Or they will become outdated and won't rank well when customers are searching for relevant reasons. For those reasons alone you need to stay on top of your items. Make sure you are constantly refreshing them or relisting them if necessary. If you listing isn't visible to potential customers then you will never sell the item and make the money.

Chapter 7 - Sniping items on Craigslist to resell on craigslist

When I first got started selling on craigslist I was doing a lot of this. It's amazing how many items are undervalued on craigslist by uninformed sellers. If you are educated, have a specialized niche, or just know your stuff, you can make a lot of money buying items on craigslist and then going back and reselling them on craigslist too. One of my best secrets for sniping items on craigslist is to be the first one to respond to a new listing.

Check out this tool below I use to do so.

Pretty much in a nutshell the tool sets up personalized alerts. It's very effective because it allows you to save time by going about your day without constantly scanning the newly listed items on craigslist. When you set up an alert it will notify you via email when an item with certain keywords newly appears on the site.

=====.> **Click Here To Check Out the FREE Tool**

If you don't want to set up alerts than I would advise you constantly refresh the newly listed items for sale within a given category.

I would do this for bicycles and would spend 4-5 hours a day "Sniping items".

I'm telling you there is a lot of money to be made on craigslist; Try it out!

Chapter 8- Creating a Vision/Plan for Your Business and follow through on it

Now that you are starting to acquire handfuls of quality inventory for a good price you now have to create a vision/plan for your business. And on top of that, you need to figure out how you will execute and make things happen!

With that in mind, I am going to create a sample plan for you to follow or tailor to your own needs based on selling $2,000 a month on craigslist

Plan and Execution

- I will go sourcing three times a week for 2 hours a day (M/W/F)
- I will dedicate a few hours twice a week or picture all my items I need to list
- I will list 5 items a day Monday through Friday
- I will spend 30 minutes a day studying the sold and completed listings on eBay and craiglist, Monday through Friday for 3 months straight

- I will spend 15 minutes a day three times a week watching helpful YouTube videos that allow me to learn new items to resell
- I will spend 30 minutes a day meeting up with potential customers

Again the plan and execution example above is just a sample and will have to be tailored to your own needs and goals but I hope you see where I am going. Based on my sales I have found that listing 15-25 highly profitable items a week over the long haul has allowed me to easily sell $2,000 a month on craigslist. Of course this may differ for you depending on the types of items you are selling, and the average sale you are receiving, but again this is just a sample to get you thinking. It is very important you formulate a plan and a means to execute so you can achieve your goal. This is what will separate the winner's from the losers!

Chapter 9- Scaling Up to $2,000+ a month on craigslist

Putting systems in place will make or break you when you are running a craigslist business. If you want to scale up to $2,000 a month or more on craigslist you will need to have a system in place for cleaning inventory, storing inventory, relisting items, editing pictures, listing items, managing employees (if you have them), meeting with customers, and the list goes on and on.

I am not going to go into major detail in terms of specific systems and how to create one, but I want to drill in your head why it is so important to have them.

Having systems in place for everything you do in your business will allow for things to run much more smoothly and will enable you to scale your business even bigger when the time is right.

If you want to figure out how to put the proper systems in place all you need to do is break down all of your daily tasks. Take a look at your method for storing your inventory and ask yourself, "Is this method efficient, can I improve this system anyway"? Doing this will give you some great ideas and will get your started on the right path to creating systems or better systems.

Trust me if you want to make $2,000 a month or more on craigslist you will need systems in place!

As an example, one system I have in place has to do with my employee that works for me. What I do is I give my worker a stack of about 30 papers each Monday before he starts picturing the items that I will be listing each week. Each paper is known as a listing template and has the necessary information I would like him to fill out. By creating this system or otherwise known as a listing template it has allowed my employee to save time and become more efficient. This is an example of a system that saves time and saves me money!

Start thinking of how you can create systems!

If you want to earn $2,000 a month or more on craigslist I believe it is extremely smart to hire an employee. An employee can be great because it can allow you to delegate tasks off that are not required of you to do personally, and will allow you to free up time to spend on other more important projects.

When it comes to making money on craigslist one of the greatest uses of your time will be out sourcing quality inventory.

While taking pictures, listing items, measuring items, cleaning items, meeting with customers, and so on it extremely important, in the big picture it does not make you money. In my opinion the money is made when you buy an item, and you need to spend as much time as possible looking for those items at thrift stores, auctions, yard sales, flea markets, and craigslist so you can make a ton of money in your craigslist business.

So now that you know why you need an employee how in the world are you going to hire one? Well, from my personal experience I have hired a few friends, college students, retirees, and some random folks off of craigslist. So first thing I would suggest is talking to some friends and see if anyone is looking for some extra cash.

If you can't find any friends interested then I would look at the other options. Probably one of the easiest ways to do this would be to make a craigslist ad. In today's economy there are a ton of people looking for work and it is quite easy to find people. The key is finding good people that you can trust and do a good job. This will take some time!

A quick tip of advice when hiring people, try to only hire someone for a specific task. For example hire one person for taking pictures, another for listing items and another for sourcing items. I have found if you hire someone to do it all they will eventually leave you and do what you are doing their self!

Conclusion

Thank you again for downloading the book "Craigslist: How to make $2,000+ Every Month Working from Home Part- Time on Craigslist." I hope this book was able to help to get started selling on craigslist, and eventually scaling your business to the point of earning $2,000+ a month on a consistent continual basis.

The next step is to start taking action on the information you have absorbed and come up with a plan that will guide you towards success. Remember education is key, so keep referring back to this book to continually level up your business.

Finally, if you enjoyed this book, please take the time to share your thoughts and post a review on Amazon. It'd be greatly appreciated! Thank you and good luck!

Book # 3

Thrift Store

How to Earn $3000+ Every Month Selling Easy to Find Items From Thrift Stores, Garage Sales, and Flea Markets

Copyright © 2015

All rights reserved. No part of this book may be reproduced in any form without permission in writing from the author. Reviewers may quote brief passages in reviews.

Disclaimer

No part of this publication may be reproduced or transmitted in any form or by any means, mechanical or electronic, including photocopying or recording, or by any information storage and retrieval system, or transmitted by email without permission in writing from the publisher.

While all attempts and efforts have been made to verify the information held within this publication, neither the author nor the publisher assumes any responsibility for errors, omissions, or opposing interpretations of the content herein.

This book is for entertainment purposes only. The views expressed are those of the author alone, and should not be taken as expert instruction or commands. The reader of this book is responsible for his or her own actions when it comes to reading the book.

Adherence to all applicable laws and regulations, including international, federal, state, and local governing professional licensing, business practices, advertising, and all other aspects of doing business in the US, Canada, or any other jurisdiction is the sole responsibility of the purchaser or reader.

Neither the author nor the publisher assumes any responsibility or liability whatsoever on the behalf of the purchaser or reader of these materials.

Any received slight of any individual or organization is purely unintentional.

Table of Contents

Introduction

Chapter 1 - Financial Independence

Chapter 2 - Thrift Stores, Garage Sales, and Flea Markets. Oh my!

Chapter 3 - Discovering Your Niche

Chapter 4 - Consumer Hunting

Chapter 5 - Effectively Describing Items

Chapter 6 - Growing Profits to a Steady Income

Conclusion

Introduction

I want to thank you and congratulate you for downloading the book, "Thrift Store - How to Earn $3,000+ Every Month Selling Easy to Find Items From Thrift Stores, Garage Sales, and Flea Markets".

This book contains proven steps and strategies for earning $3,000+ every month selling easy to find items.

If you take the time to read this book fully and apply the information held within this book will help you to achieve financial freedom!

Thanks again for downloading this book, I hope you enjoy it!

Chapter 1: Financial Independence

So you want to become financially independent? Are you sick and tired of waking up in the morning, commuting through traffic, dealing with that horrible boss, and making other people filthy rich? People live most of their lives rushing to the punch-in clock day in and day out without any end in sight. It's no secret that not all of these people are happy with their lives. There is a much easier way to make a living in this slow economy and achieve pure financial freedom.

What if I told you there is a proven way for you to achieve complete financial freedom and live a truly happy and peaceful life? You could say goodbye to your dead-end job, work your own hours, be your own boss, and spend your time the way you want to spend it. Would you be interested in knowing this secret? Of course you would be, that is why you bought this book.

As with any proven method, it will take time, determination and effort to achieve absolute financial independence. Nothing in this world comes easy, so you will have to work to find the methods that best suit your situation. You are already off to a great start.

First of all, you must be and remain motivated. Take out a sheet of paper and write a brief paragraph on why you need to change your financial situation. Write another brief paragraph on the financial goals you expect to achieve. As you go through this book, write down how you are going to do it. Each day, take a look at this piece of paper until you have achieved your goal. Then burn or shred that piece of paper because you will no longer have to look back.

You may not have much money to start out with and that is absolutely fine. You may feel like a small fish in a big pond at first. That is the amazing part about starting out a venture such as this one. As long as youexactly follow exactly what we say here, by the time you reach chapter 6: Compounding Profits for a Steady Income, you will possess the information to turn yourself into a much bigger fish.

We will explore methods that will help you find and sell ordinary items at thrift stores, garage sales, and flea markets. All the information is literally at your fingertips. Remember that the moretime and effort you put into these working methods the more successful you will be.

Chapter 2: Thrift Stores, Garage Sales, and Flea Markets. Oh My!

The key to any successful financial endeavor is to find a need and fill it. In this chapter we will explore the many places you can find many goods that people will need. The amount capital you start with will determine how fast you will achieve your goal. You may start right now with almost nothing and build up your own business buying and selling secondhand goods.

We are a society of consumers that rely on supply and demand. The more in demand a product may be in your area, the easier it will be to sell. The smaller the supply of a product that is in demand, the more profit you can make. You have to be in the right place at the right time to find valuable stock to sell to your consumers.

We will speak more about consumers in Chapter 4: Consumer Hunting. For now, we need to focus on your stock; the product you will be marketing and selling.

Thrift Stores, Garage Sales, and Flea Markets are packed with secondhand "junk" that people no longer need or want. Even though they may have bought these products brand new at quadruple the price, they have depreciated in value. People are willing to part with these products that they, at one time, adored and are now willing to accept a very small amount of money from someone who will want them. Let's explore each one of these types of places where you can find secondhand goods.

1. Thrift Stores:

Thrift Stores can be found almost anywhere. You may already be familiar with the ones in or around your area. They are places that receive unwanted goods from people. Typically, they use the proceeds from the sales of these items for a charitable cause. This is where you will find anything from normal household objects to old overlooked vintage antique items that could be highly sought after.

Since these places rely mostly on donations, they have an almost unlimited stock of various items from the people in that area. Sometimes when people pass away they or their families may donate part or all of their belongings to a thrift store. This can be a hotspot for overlooked valuables.

How to find a good thrift store:

Using this method, you will find a thrift store that will have the most valuable goods at the prices you are willing to pay.

Begin with searching on whichever search engine you prefer. My preference is http://www.google.com so I will use that one as an example. Most if not all search engines have a local directory these days, so feel free to use your own.

Simply type in "Thrift Store" and click "Search". On Google, you will receive millions of results. Since we will want to look locally we will go to the top menu and click on "maps". You may have to put in your zip code to see results in your area.

Your results will be narrowed down to a much smaller number of thrift stores in your area. Navigate around the map or search through the listings in the areas you are looking in.

To determine which thrift stores you should be looking for, you should have a good idea on what type of capital you are working with. Try not to be intimidated by the word capital. It is just a fancy way of saying money; it is the amount of money you have available for use. In this case, the amount of money you have available to buy goods for resale.

You have no capital:

If you are starting out with little or no capital, there's still a way for you to start making money! Some thrift stores will take your unwanted items and give you a credit towards a purchase in their store. You should call around and ask which ones will do this. They don't care what types of items as long as they are sellable. It's time for you to go through the attic and garage. If you haven't seen it for over a year, you should part with it. You may be killing two birds with one stone because you'll probably need the storage for the items you are going to buy and sell.

You have low capital:

Look for thrift stores in low-income areas. These stores will be marketed towards lower income families. There, you will be able to find lower quality goods from donations given by lower-income families. Items here are sold at very low prices.

You have slightly higher capital:

Look for thrift stores in middle class-income areas. These stores will be marketed towards families with slightly higher incomes. There, you will be able to find moderate quality goods from donations given by middleclass families. Items here are sold at slightly higher prices.

You have very high capital:

Look for thrift stores in or around high class properties and high income residents. You will know the type of area in which to look by its appearance; they have gates at the front of their driveways, a lot of property, and help (maids, butlers, gardeners).

These stores will be marketed towards families on the middle class and higher-income fence.There, you will be able to find every kind of good including a lot of high quality goods at a fraction of the price.

Remember: When looking for products in thrift stores take the time to look through the whole store before picking any items for purchase to avoid impulse buying. No matter how great the item is, remember to keep your own impulses out of the equation. Eventually, you'll be able to buy any of these items and you'll probably be able to get a better deal for yourself in the future.

2. Garage Sales:

Garage sales can be very easy to find and not a challenge for most. They can be a great opportunity to find good quality items at low prices. The best part is that there are usually no taxes.

You can find them in almost any residential area if you just drive around. People usually have them during the weekends, and when the weather is good.

Another good part about garage sales is that the seller is usually negotiable on the prices. They could be desperate and willing to let anything go for as much as half of the selling price. The best way to negotiate would be to strike up a friendly conversation. This can be really easy if you are a real people person. Simply say "I would love this item, but I cannot spend this much on it. Would you consider letting it go for "this lower amount". Make up an excuse if you have to, maybe there is a small scuff mark on the coffee table you're interested in and it would cost you money to repair it. It works a lot more than you'd think. Most of these people just want these items out of their house.

How to find a good garage sale:

Search through your local newspapers where you can find garage sale listings in the local classifieds.

Look through http://www.craigslist.org in your particular state and county to find garage sale listings.

Be on the lookout for fliers posted on telephone poles and bulletin boards at supermarkets.

Look out for Moving or Estate sales. These should be at the top of your list. These are sales that happen when the people cannot take the items with them.

If you happen to miss one of these and you're in the area anyway be sure to check the curb for any goods that may be put out for garbage for a free item. Remember that most people just want them out of their sight and out of their house!

Again, you Garage Sale of choice will depend on the amount of capital you have.

You have low capital:

Look for garage sales located in low-income residential areas. Here, you will find low-mid quality goods at a very low price. Most of the people having garage sales in these areas arestrapped for cash and will take anything you'll give them. Low ball offers accepted. Haggle away.

You have slightly higher capital:

Look for garage sales located in middle class areas. Here, you will find mid-high quality goods at a low price. The people in these areas are harder to haggle with. That should not stop you from trying. Even if you can get five dollars off of that awesome ride on lawnmower and you know someone will pay you another ten dollars over that amount, do it! Every little bit will add up, I promise!

You have very high capital:

There won't be many garage sales but you may be lucky! Your best bet is to search for estate sales in high end areas. Estate sales will help you find very high quality goods for a fraction of the price. This is where you'll find the good stuff! Search for those sought after items. Haggling may be difficult in these areas but let's hope you have enough experience at this point to know that almost anything is negotiable.

3. Flea Markets:

Flea markets are another place where you can find secondhand and brand new goods. A flea market is a place where the owner rents out "booths" or "stalls" where the vendor can set up shop and sell all sorts of items. Here, you will find various items at various prices. I will only recommend that you have a slightly higher to very high capital when purchasing these items.

You will find that flea markets get really busy with people looking for a good deal during any time of the year. There are rules you should follow when bargain hunting at a flea market. These people are trying to make money just like you are trying to.

Do not criticize the prices or products. These people make a living haggling. Everything here is negotiable. This is great for establishing relationships with vendors for future purchases. Be nice, courteous, and feel free to make friends here.

Do not let them hear you criticize a price or product out loud. It's disrespectful and they will not want to please a person who disrespects the way they make a living, so be friendly and respectful.

Here's a tip: Play the game. Ask to look at a product or ask for additional information about it. Such as where is it made or what the material it is made from. Seem interested and spend some time with the product. Then look or ask about the price. Use a facial expression that tells them that you will pass on the purchase. You'll find that the vendor will immediately drop the price to make a sale.

Trash = Treasure:

Another man's trash is another man's treasure. That's where you come in. Find a person who needs an item that you have and sell it to them. You will discover that you are not finding trash or junk. In the end you have become a treasure hunter.

Chapter 3: Finding Your Niche

You don't want to become overwhelmed in holding various products and not being able to sell them. You will need to find your niche. A niche is a particular type of items in a market. When you're confident with one niche, you may explore others. However, it's important to find one and stick with it at the beginning.

Start with the products that you know the most about. Perhaps you are a parent and you are experienced in buying baby and kid's clothes. Maybe you know a lot about electronics because you've been into them since you were a kid. If you are a musician, you may know a little or a lot about musical instruments. These are just examples. It is up to you to figure out what type of product will be the easiest for you to buy in confidence you are getting the best deal. In this chapter, we will go through the various items you will find in thrift stores and how they might relate to your particular niche.

Staying and continuing to sell in a niche will give you a reputation for being a great seller of that particular type of item. The best advertising is word of mouth. You will become more experienced in buying these particular items and increase your profits.

Remember to keep seasons and holidays in mind. Buy items that are out of season at a very low price and sell them right before the season starts for a good long-term profit. Try your hardest to sell on hand products as last minute holiday gifts.

Clothing and Shoes:

Everybody wears shoes and clothes. You already have experience in this if you wear clothes. What you may think is ugly or unfashionable could be beautiful and chic in someone else's eyes. It is best that you do become familiar with current trends, but it is not required when buying and selling these items.

Thrift Stores, Garage Sales, and Flea Markets are packed with secondhand clothing and shoes. When you look around these places, you will find that there is an almost unlimited supply of:

Baby Clothes and Shoes –

These are needed items for babies all year 'round and they are plentiful. Supply is high and demand is high. Buy as much as you can in various sizes, styles, and seasons. More than 300,000 babies are born in the US every year, and they need clothes. Moreover, growing babies go through a lot of cloths in different sizes. For this reason, consumers looking for a good deal do not want to spend an arm and a leg on an item that their babies will ruin or grow out of. Your profits will be low per item so you will need to sell a lot to see a good overall profit from these items.

Kids Clothes and Shoes –

Just like babies, kids go through clothes and shoes really fast. Buy a moderate amount of items that are in style. These items will cost a bit more than baby items but will still be cheap. Like babies, kids are constantly ruining clothes and shoes and they grow out of them fast! Profits should be moderate on each item sold.

Women's Clothes and Shoes –

Women generally know what they want, especially women who want a good deal. You're going to have to have a woman's mind or learn about the current styles to do well with these items. They will not be cheap, so hold out for those good deals. Shoes and boots are items that some women love. I would suggest buying a very moderate amount of shoes and clothing for women. Profits can be huge if you know what you're doing, but the sales will not be as easy.

Men's Clothes and Shoes –

The average male can be a very picky shopper for clothes. You're going to have to do some research on the latest trends to sell well with these items. They will not be extremely cheap, so hold out for those really good deals. A good tip, here, would be to learn the newest sneaker trends, sneaker heads can be impulse buyers. Try to stick to the items men might need such as boots, dress shoes, suits, and ties that are in good shape in various sizes. Buy a moderate amount of these. Profits can be huge but may be a harder sell.

A tip for long-term profits from shoes and clothing:

Buy those cute warm jackets in the summertime or summer clothes in the winter. They will be very cheap because they are out of season, especially when it comes to babies' or kids' items. Pack them away until the fall or spring for a long-term investment. They will sell fast and profitably.

Clothing Accessories -

You should purchase these items if you are going to sell clothing. Some accessories for clothing include: handbags, umbrellas, canes, ties, hats, belts, gloves, earmuffs, scarves, socks, stockings, etc... These items can be found in thrift stores, garage sales, and flea markets for cheap. You will find them in various sizes and styles.

Toys and Games:

We've all been children and some of you may have children. So we know that children are impulse buyers. They just don't want toys, they need them. As a result, parents also become impulse buyers when they are buying toys and games. You will find these items at almost all thrift stores, garage sales, and flea markets.

Some of the items you may find will probably be: board games, action figures, radio controlled vehicles, coloring books, dolls, stuffed animals, science toys, models, puzzles, play sets, cars, trucks, etc...The list is almost endless.

It is important that you inspect these items as most second hand toys run a high risk of being damaged, incomplete, or worn from children playing with them. Inspect that each item contains all pieces, is clean, and works correctly before purchasing. If the item takes batteries, check the compartment they should be in for evidence of corrosion. These items may be resealed inside of a box. Just ask permission from the seller for you to look and inspect the item before purchasing.

This is a great niche as long as you buy and sell good quality products. You can find these items relatively cheap and make great profits on them.

Electronics and Video Games:

This niche can be tricky if you do not know exactly what you're looking for. This is not a need in any sense, so when people are shopping for electronics and video games, they are searching for an item that they want.

In thrift stores, garage sales, and flea markets you may find: video game consoles, video games, alarm clocks, televisions, DVD/blue ray players, VCR players, stereo systems, cameras, video cameras, laptops/computers, portable audio players, phone, cell phones, and various other gadgets.

Be on the lookout for highly sought after items such as vintage video games, antique radios, and anything old that may be a collector's item that will bring you the big bucks.

It is important that you inspect these items and be sure they are not damaged and are in proper working order. There is a wide range of consumers looking for these products and it's a buyer's market. Meaning you would have to expect competition in this niche. If you buy the right items at the right prices, your profits can be great in this niche, but you need to have enough background information going in.

Appliances:

This niche is great if you have a good amount of capital. There is a want and a need for appliances in the US, where we have been accustomed to using them in our everyday lives. Keep in mind that you may need a large vehicle to transport and a place to store most of these items. The more you know about these items, especially if you can fix them, the easier they will be for you to sell.

In most thrift stores, garage sales, and flea markets, you may find: air conditioners, lamps, fans, electronic can openers, toasters, washers & dryers, dishwashers, stoves, electric griddles, irons, refrigerators, electronic space heaters, and much more!

It is very important that these items are safe. Be sure they are not damaged, and that they are in complete working order before you decide to sell them. If you hold out for really good prices on these items, the profits can be huge!

Furniture:

This niche can be very profitable. Keep in mind these items are mostly huge, so you will need a large vehicle for transporting furniture as well as a place to store them.

The more you know about these items, the easier they will be for you to buy and sell. The great thing about furniture is that they may be sold in sets at a lower price. Be on the lookout for vintage pieces that may be worth a lot of money!

Some of the furniture items you will find at thrift stores, garage sales, and flea markets include: tables, chairs, benches, couches, pool tables, cupboards, chests, wall units, beds, wardrobes, and much more. They will come in various styles and they'll be made of many materials such as wood, glass, and metals.

Most of these items will bear some type of damage from being used. It is important that you learn how to cover up scratches and be able to repair these items so you may resell them for a higher price than what you paid.

You may need a large amount of capital to buy these items and it may take time to sell them but your profits can be plentiful.

Pet Items:

Some see pet items as a necessity for their pets because they simply love them. This niche can be very profitable depending on how you market the products (we will get into that later in Chapter 4: Consumer Hunting).

Some of these items you'll be able to find at thrift stores, garage sales, and flea markets, but you will probably have a hard time finding a steady and good supply of them. The items that you should be looking for include: Cages, grooming supplies, harnesses & leashes, pet toys, feeders, beds, collars, tanks, and anything else that is pet related.

If these items are second hand, you want to make sure that they are clean and safe for pets. The people who are going to buy these items from you love their pets, so keep a good reputation and they may come back to buy more items.

You may need a moderate sized capital for this niche. As long as you can find a steady supply of goods at great prices you can do very well with pet items.

Everything Else:

Those were just a few good examples of the various types of items you can choose to buy and sell. When you walk into a thrift store, visit a garage sale, or take a trip to the flea market you'll find just about anything! Be on the lookout for items that people will want or need.

It's important that you find a niche because you need to build experience and a reputation in selling a particular type of item. The experience will help you market the item and sell it easily. Selling random items may wind up consuming every storage space you have available and eating away at your capital. Organization will be important in this part of the process. As your capital grows, you may move on to better and more profitable niches.

Chapter 4: Consumer Hunting

We are all consumers. If you bought this eBook, you are a consumer. Anyone who buys anything is a consumer. What does this tell us? Well for one, we are everywhere. This makes the hunt quite easy and simple.

In order to hunt for a consumer, you'll have to think like a consumer. Who are they buying an item for, what kind of item do they want, where can they buy this item, when can they receive this item, why should they buy this item, and how much will they spend?

In this chapter, we will discover the many hunting grounds where you will find your consumers. The chase can be frustrating and tedious, but you must be willing to put yourself out there to make the sale.

There are many free and inexpensive ways to promote the sale of your items. You can sell items right from home easily. You may also meet potential buyers in a public place such as a parking lot in front of a local convenience store. You may also arrange to send an item to a seller's address.

There are some precautions you should keep in mind. Be sure to use the proper precautions when meeting a seller face to face. Always make sure, in advance, the seller will have the correct amount of money if paying in cash so you won't need to bring change. Only meet in a brightly lit public area. Bring a friend or family member to help you complete a transaction if you are unsure. It is better to be safe than sorry.

Promote your item physically:

List your items in local classifieds in the local newspapers or Penny saver advertisement papers. This may cost you some money, but it is an effective way to sell items that people need, especially at the beginning before you establish a customer base.

Post flyers around town. I'm sure you've seen flyers posted before. Use the telephone poles, supermarket bulletin boards, or anywhere that you are allowed to legally post a flyer.

Promote your item virtually:

Use http://www.craigslist.org to post your item online for the people who are searching for good deals on items in your area.Use the wanted section to give you a good idea on the types of items that are in demand.

Use http://www.ebay.com to auction or sell your item globally. This is the largest marketplace for used items, and it is very well-known. Take note that there are selling and shipping fees that are applied to items listed on this site, and that you must use a registered and approved account to list an item on eBay.

Use http://www.amazon.com to sell your item globally. This is a great place to sell used items. Take note that there are selling and shipping fees that are applied to items listed on this site, and that you must use a registered and approved account to list on Amazon.

Use http://www.facebook.com to sell your item locally. Yes, that's right; Facebook can help you sell your items. If you are unfamiliar with this concept, we will explain it to you. If you have a Facebook account, there will be groups you can join to sell your item. At the top of the page type in "sell" and hit the search button. Then click "groups" under the "more" tab. You will find local groups that have thousands of members that will see your ad when you post it. Click "add" next to as many groups as you want and wait for your approval before posting. It's very easy and simple to use.You may even find people asking for items, so be sure to pay attention to them.Best of all, it's absolutely free! Be sure to read and abide by all the rules of every group.

These are the best ways to promote your item and get thousands of eyes on your stock. You may use any of these items in conjunction with each other and cancel all other listings after you have found your buyer. Be sure to read all the rules and realize that there may be a fee for pulling an item from sites such as eBay. You should also be aware that sales sometimes fall through. It happens. Just relist and keep moving on.

Once you have made contact with a buyer, be sure to be nice and courteous; be the best seller you can possibly be. You should know a great amount about your niche by now, so start up a conversation about the piece that is being sold and suggest a similar item that you have on hand to make another sale right away. The worst that can happen is for the buyer tosay no.

If the buyers seem pleased with the service you offered, let them know that you will be getting more items very soon and to ask them to let anyone else who might be looking for a similar item to come to you.

Chapter 5: Effectively Describing Items

So you know what you're selling, where to buy your items, who to sell them to, and where to list them. Do you know how to effectively describe and sell your item? In this chapter, we will show you how to effectively describe your item.

Get rid of the guesswork for the buyer right off the bat. In order to effectively describe your item, you must provide a brief and detailed description of the item you are trying to sell. The more detailed your description is, the better luck you will have selling it.

State exactly what the item is that you're selling. You may want to do some research on the general aspects of the product. State the name, model, and manufacturer of the product as the title. In the brief description, list the details such as:

- Year it was made.
- Materials it is made from.
- The condition it is in.
- Size/Dimensions.

- Color of the item.

- If the item is used or not.

Avoid selling products that may be illegal in your state/county. Even though you may have bought it legally, it doesn't mean you can sell it legally. If you are unsure, then you should check with local laws.

Don't use any information in the description of your item that isn't true. Try to be as brief as possible without leaving any details out of the description.

Chapter 6: Growing Profits to a Steady Income

After learning how to buy items, how to market them and how to sell them to potential clients, you hopefully started making a good profit. This is not the end of the road, however. Hold on for one more moment before you spend a single penny. If you spend your profit now, you'll have to start the whole process over to get it back. You need a way to reach your goal of $3000+ per month.

You must have a strong willpower to not spend a single cent until your profits reach your goal each month. You must let it ride in order to grow your profits.

The reason behind this is simple. You're going to take your initial capital we'll call that (C). Then, we will take your profit and call that (P). Once your profit (P) minus your initial capital (C) equals your goal (G) you will have reached the financial freedom you've worked so hard for.

C – P = G

Example:

Let's say you start out with $50, an easily obtainable capital. If you can double that by your first month you will have $100. At the start of your second month you will have $100 (C+P) to buy used goods. If you can double that, you'll have $200 to invest in the third month. By the end of month three you should have $400. If you add your capital to your profit each month by the end of the 6th month you will have made $3200. If you continue after that you may start spending your profit.

C x 2 = P will be the result at the end of each month.

Month 1 = $100, Month 2 = $200, Month 3 = $400

Month 4 = $800 Month 5 = $1600 Month 6 = $3200

By month 6, you will have made $3150 profit. $3200 (C-P). As long as you keep using all of the money you made from month 6 you'll hold the same profits each month after. At 7 months, you will continue to pull in 3000+ each month.The more money you start with the faster you will achieve your goals. Good Luck!

Conclusion

Thank you again for downloading this book!

I hope this book was able to help you to earn $3000+ each month.

The next step is to get out there and start making money!

Finally, if you enjoyed this book, please take the time to share your thoughts and post a review on Amazon. It'd be greatly appreciated!

Thank you and good luck!

Book # 4

Garage Sales

The Ultimate Beginner's Guide to Making Killer Profits from Garage Sales in 30 Minutes or Less!

Copyright © 2015

All rights reserved. No part of this book may be reproduced in any form without permission in writing from the author. Reviewers may quote brief passages in reviews.

Disclaimer

No part of this publication may be reproduced or transmitted in any form or by any means, mechanical or electronic, including photocopying or recording, or by any information storage and retrieval system, or transmitted by email without permission in writing from the publisher.

While all attempts and efforts have been made to verify the information held within this publication, neither the author nor the publisher assumes any responsibility for errors, omissions, or opposing interpretations of the content herein.

This book is for entertainment purposes only. The views expressed are those of the author alone, and should not be taken as expert instruction or commands. The reader of this book is responsible for his or her own actions when it comes to reading the book.

Adherence to all applicable laws and regulations, including international, federal, state, and local governing professional licensing, business practices, advertising, and all other aspects of doing business in the US, Canada, or any other jurisdiction is the sole responsibility of the purchaser or reader.

Neither the author nor the publisher assumes any responsibility or liability whatsoever on the behalf of the purchaser or reader of these materials.

Any received slight of any individual or organization is purely unintentional.

Contents

Introduction

Chapter 1: Garage Sale Basics

Chapter 2: When to organize a garage sale

Chapter 3: How to Properly Price Your Items

Chapter 3: Garage Sale Ads

Chapter 4: Rules and Tips For Successful Garage Sale

Chapter 5: Why are Garage Sales Profitable for Buyers Too

Chapter 6: Garage Sale Fun Facts

Conclusion

Introduction

First and foremost, I want to thank you for downloading the book, "Garage Sales – The Ultimate Beginner's Guide to Making Killer Profits from Garage Sales in 30 Minutes or Less!".

In this book you will learn how to plan your own garage sale. Also, you will learn all the steps you will need to take before you display the items you are selling for people to purchase. Garage sales are the only way of getting rid of the stuff you don't want or need anymore, it is great a way of earning money, connecting with people and teaching your children some responsibility.

This Garage sale basics book will teach you more about the concept of holding a garage sale, in addition all the reasons why people decide to have one. Additionally, this book will teach you when is the right time of year, the day, and time to organize your garage sale in order to gain more profits.

You don't have to worry about how you are going to price your items, because this book contains a special section where you will learn how to set a price for certain items, baby clothes, adult clothing, furniture, antiques, decorative items, electronics and kitchen appliances. Further, you will learn more about how to properly price your items and how to track your sales correctly.

Garage sales simply can't be successful without flyers and advertisements, therefore this book will teach you how to write the perfect ad and flyer that will attract more visitors, and what to include, and what not to include.

Basic garage sale tips, advice and tricks are included here so you will know how to conduct your garage sale and how to treat the people who attend.

To make things more interesting, this book contains fun facts about the history of garage sales.

Thanks again for downloading this book, I hope you enjoy it!

Chapter 1: Garage Sale Basics

Garage sales have been part of our culture and tradition for hundreds of years, however most people miss all of the fun in being a part of garage sales (buyers + sellers). There is more to it then to just buying and selling items. Garage sales are opportunities to bring people together while still making money or finding that special item you have always wanted.

The purpose of this book is to explain the concept of garage sales and to teach you how to make a big profits for yourself.

What is a Garage Sale

Garage sales are informal events where people sell their used goods. Sellers at garage sales are not required to have a business license or need to collect sales tax.

Garage sales are also known by the terms, yard sale, junk sale, attic sale, or basement sale.

Items that can be found at garage sales include books, toys, clothes, furniture, sports equipment, kitchen appliances etc. Basically, everything someone no longer needs can be included in their garage sale.

Why to Hold a Garage Sale

Garage sales can be organized for several reasons and they include:

- Eliminating things a person no longer wants or need anymore – garage sales are perfect events for people to finally get rid of clothing and furniture that you no longer need. Also, if your children have grown up, there really is no need to keep their baby clothes, or toys. So instead of keeping them in your attic or basement, you can actually profit from selling these items.

- Make someone happy – believe it or not, there are people who love buying used stuff at garage sales. These people are bargain and treasure hunters, and they like old stuff, and sometimes garage sales offer things they are unable to find at the store. Organizing a garage sale is the perfect way to make someone happy and earn you some money along the way.

- Earn money – well, who says garage sales can't make you more money? Sure they can. Instead of just letting that old stuff get in your way and cluttering up your house, you can be smart, and sell them. With a smart organization technique, right pricing, and a well-written garage sale ad, you can earn more than you can imagine.

- Make space for things you care about – selling stuff you don't need is a perfect way to make room in your home for the things you do love. First, your house, including the attic and basement will be clutter-free, basically anywhere you are storing things you don't need. Second, you get to conduct a little makeover of your house. You will make room for the new things you want, because you will now have all the free space you need.

- Meeting new people – garage sales are perfect occasions to meet your neighbors, and new people. Additionally, you will meet bargain hunters who will inform you about other garage sales where you might find something you would like. If you're new in the neighborhood, this is a perfect opportunity to meet your neighbors, and get to know them better.

- Fund-raising – people often throw a garage sale to raise money for a certain causes. It is a win-win situation – you get rid of the stuff you don't want or need anymore, and along the way you are able to help someone.

- Purchasing other stuff – unfortunatly you can't earn millions of dollars, but the money you do gain from your garage sales can and will help you purchase something else you want, but possibly didn't have enough funds to get before.

- Teaching kids about business and responsibility – garage sales are ideal for parents who want to teach their children how to conduct a business, and how to be responsible with their money. It's a perfect way to show them the value of a dollar, and how hard work, and being wise pays off. Not only that, you are also teaching them to respect other people (customers), and to respect other stuff around the house (as you might need them to help you organize your next garage sale).

Chapter 2: When to organize a garage sale

If you want your garage sale to be successful and to make a significant amount of money, then it is important to pick the best date and time for the event.

Naturally, garage sales require careful organization. You cannot just decide to throw the event, take your stuff out and hope for the best. Your goal is making money, and it won't come without the right schedule, careful consideration, and thorough planning.

Throughout this chapter, we will talk about organizing the garage sale and picking the right month, date, and time of your event.

Let's face it, everything revolves around careful planning and having the right organization. If you want to make a killer profit by selling things you don't use anymore, then you need a detailed plan about what time of the year is the best for your garage sale, what day of the week will get the most profit, and when should your garage sale open and close.

Your entire profit doesn't only depend on the things that people buy, but it also depends on the right timing.

Timing is the factor that can either make, or break your garage sale and its profit.

If you are a first-time seller, pay close attention to our advice for choosing the best time to hold your garage sale.

Best Month

Considering you will need to move all of your stuff outside, and stay outside until your garage sale is over, the best time of the year for a garage sale is during spring.

Spring is ideal because unlike winter there aren't cold temperatures, and snow.

Early spring garage sales are the most popular, it is also the time when you are able to earn more money.

If you're not a fan of spring, or simply can't organize everything at that time, then your next best opportunity is the second Saturday in August. It is also known as National Garage Sale Day. Summer garage sales are also popular, and throwing one on the National Garage sale day can guarantee the most money.

FUN FACT: National Garage Sale Day is an idea started in 2001 by C. Daniel Rhodes from Alabama. He noticed his neighbors had garage sales on different weekends, and realized everyone would make more profit if garage sales were held on the same day.

Garage sales thrown at the end of summer can be as successful as those in early spring. So, if you want to throw a garage sale, make sure you pick early spring or late summer. Additonally, when you choose the month, it is always best to have garage sale at the beginning of that month. It will make more money than garage sales held at the end of the month.

Best Day

When you decide the time of the year and the month of your garage sale, it is important to choose what time it will be. Naturally, week days are not a good idea because people work during the week, they are also busy and simply don't have time to visit various garage sales. And let's face it, you might have a job too, or you have to pick up your kids from school, so week days are not also good for you.

The best days for garage sales are Friday, Saturday, and Sunday.

Friday – is good if your home is located near any busy roads during lunch or after work.

Saturday – is always the best day to throw a garage sale. Most people have their best sales on Saturdays. They have enough time to organize everything, people whom come are generally off of work and have the time to visit different garage sales.

Sunday – are not as profitable as Saturdays. But there is significant traffic, and Sundays are usually the day when people are on the hunt to find a specific item. There are people who visit garage sales every Sunday to look for items that can't be bought anywhere else.

The Bottom line is, if you want your garage sale to be successful, try to organize it on Saturday as that is the most profitable day for your event.

Garage sales on Friday and Sunday should be organized when:

- You have a specific or hard-to-find item that you want to sell
- If Friday or Sunday is an "open house" day in your neighborhood, (it's usually Sunday)

- If your garage sale is multi-day sale.

Best Time

If you want your garage sale to be successful (and you do), then you can't obviously start at noon. Even though garage sales are held during weekends, one might think there is no need to hurry as people choose that time to sleep in. That is wrong.

The busiest time for the garage sale is between 7AM and 11AM. Also, that period of time can determine the success of your sale for the remainder of the day.

People who visit garage sales get up early and are are ready to go. Hence, the earlier you start, the more successful it will be. People often find they begin taking items out of their homes to sale only to find a group of cars already waiting.

In order to be ready before your customers arrive and have more success, make sure your garage sale is organized and ready to start at 7AM.

REMEMBER: it is important to be organized and prepare everything early. Otherwise, you will always be step behind. Your goal is to make a killer profit with your garage sale, and that includes the proper organization.

The closing time of your garage sale should be between 1PM and 3PM.

Additional Tips for Choosing the Time and Date for Garage Sale

- April and August are the best months for holding garage sales

- Coordinate the time and date with other garage sales in your neighborhood

- Organizing a community sale in the early spring, or late summer can double or triple the number of the visitors, which also means more profit.

- When organizing, you should also check the weather forecast for that day. You don't want your garage sale ruined by poor weather.

Chapter 3: How to Properly Price Your Items

Pricing items that you want to include in your garage sale can oftentimes be challenging if you don't remember how much you paid for it originally.

Keep in mind that people who visit garage sales are there because they are hunting for bargains. They don't, and won't pay more money for something, so don't overprice items.

Pricing is an important part of your garage sale success and profit. Most people are always uncertain how to price items and think they should place a higher price on certain items. One thing is for certain, it will be easier for you after your first garage sale. You will know what items sold better, and what prices were acceptable to people.

And who said you can't make a significant profit on your first garage sale? In order to make a big profit with your very first garage sale, follow our tips about pricing.

Pricing Tips

- Baby clothes should be priced between $1 and $3. Don't price them higher, unless they are branded with the tag still attached. If they tag is still attached, we recommend pricing it up to $5.

- If the baby clothes are stained, or not in good shape then you should price them between $0.25 and $0.50 (because you just want to get rid of them anyway, plus nobody's going pay more for damaged or stained clothing).

- If you have a lot of baby clothes and you aren't sure if you will need them anymore, then you should make a special offer. For example, three baby shirts for $4 dollars, or an entire bag of baby clothes for between $5 and $10.

- Adult clothing should be priced at between $3 and $5. Make sure you don't price your old clothes higher than this, because shoppers can find them cheaper at someone else's garage sale. Plus, your goal is to make a profit and get rid of the stuff anyway. If the clothing is made by a famous brand, and still has a tag on it, then you can price it a little higher.

- Your shoes should be priced between $5 and $7.

- Price your coats between $10 and $15.

- When it comes to books, price them at $1, if the cover is beautifully designed or if the book is a rare edition, consider asking for more money. Remember, don't overprice. Your item shouldn't be as expensive or cost the same as the items sold in stores.

- If you have a lot of DVDs you want to sell, price them at $5, and CDs should be priced at $3.

- In order to sell as much as you can and get more profit, you should arrange special offers for these items also. For example, three books for $2.50, three DVDs for $10, and so on. You can even mix them up, e.g. two DVDs and one CD for $10. Be creative. Your goal is to sell as much as possible, so you have the freedom to design all kinds of special offers.

- Board games should be priced between $5 and $10.

- If you are selling old furniture that you don't need that is cluttering up your basement or attic then you should price them correctly in order to sell faster. Price furniture of low quality between $10 and $30.

- Furniture of higher quality should be priced between $50 and $75. The rule for pricing higher quality furniture for garage sales is: you should charge 1/3 of the original price. If you paid your nightstand or table $300, then you can even ask for $100 for it at your garage sale. However, if you are going to ask for 1/3 of the original price, make sure the furniture is in great condition.

- Rare antiques should be priced at $100 and more – if you have something valuable, but still want to sell it because you either don't use it anymore, don't need it, or don't have place for it, then you should start with $100. Bear in mind that you have to check the value of those items on the market. Go online and see how much items like that cost and decide on the price according to your research. Additionally, before you brand something as a rare antique, make sure it really is.

- Decorative items should be priced between $3 and $5. Items like mirrors, candlesticks, and pictures should belong in the lower-priced items at your garage sale (unless they are antiques).

- Computer equipment and some appliances should be priced at $20 or lower. Don't pay attention to how much you paid for these items, because asking for more will result in your customer leaving to find a better offer. Appliances like juicers, or toasters aren't expensive to begin with, so they can't be priced higher. Computer equipment is always changing, technology advances, so you really can't ask for more for the old equipment you don't even use anymore.

- Kitchen supplies like plates, spoons, forks etc. should be priced at between $1 and $3.

Toys should be priced between $1 and $3. Also, if you have a lot of toys, you can make special offers for them too.

Additional Pricing Tips

Along with proper pricing, you have to pay attention to the tags you place on your items, and other price-related tasks. Additional pricing tips include:

- Have your own tagging system, especially if you ask your friends and family to help you. Every person should have different colored tags.

- Even though some sellers use them, you SHOULD NOT use color-coded dot stickers. The purpose of this is to attach certain colored dot to the items, and then place the pricin chart nearby. The truth is, buyers find this system frustrating, so avoid doing it.

- Prices should be displayed large and clear.

- If you are selling paper-made items, don't use sticker tags or tape.

Don't write the price directly on the merchandice. Use tags. They are available everywhere, and are fairly inexpeinsive. The price should be on top of the merchandice, not at the bottom.

- When pricing furniture, you should use bigger tag or piece of paper to make it clear and visible.

- If there is a significant event, or special bit of information about a piece of antique furniture, or old items you want to sell, point it out, e.g. "coffee table, has been in our family since 1961"

- Point out relevant information about appliances, for example, if vacuum cleaner is corded, cordless and make sure to include what type of battery it needs if it takes batteries.

- Offer an item for free with every purchase. There are a lot of items, like toys, or if you can't sell absolutely every DVD from your collection. Buyers appreciate gifts, and make sure to point out that every buyer gets a certain item for free with their purchase. This will increase traffic and result in a good profit.

- Don't mention how you can sell the item for higher price on eBay. Let's face it, if you could, then you would have done it. And also, it's not a nice way of handling buyers at garage sales.

- Make sure items are priced the same way you'd want them to be if you decided to visit someone else's garage sale. Think this:"Would I want to buy this for this price?", if the answer is "No.", then change the price.

Chapter 3: Garage Sale Ads

If you want to make killer profits from your garage sale you need a lot of traffic. You are aware that traffic depends on the number of people that visit your garage sale, and eventually make a purchase.

People who don't live in your neighborhood and those who don't have any kind of relationship with you, can't magically know you're throwing garage sale on a certain date.

When you decide to organize your garage sale, make sure you post a lot of garage sale ads, and flyers that will inform people about the sale, location, date and time.

In this chapter, you will learn how to make your own garage sale ad that will attract a lot of people and what to put in these ads. Additionally, you will learn how to make your garage sale ad stand out and get more attention.

Good Garage Sale Ad Needs

In order to create the good garage sale ad, you have to know what the ad should include. Garage sale ads can be published online. When creating a garage sale ad you should:

- Along with online ads, consider publishing it in the local newspapers, to get more visitors
- You need to create a title that will automatically get more attention
- Create similar text for ads and flyers
- Instead of just listing the items you want to send, describe them in one sentence.
- When naming clothes, mention sizes, brands, and other information.
- Tell potential buyers why they should visit your garage sale
- Be honest about the items' condition. Don't make this information up, and don't sugar-coat anything. People understand that items at garage sales are used and not in perfect condition, so just be honest.
- Try to include a couple of photos

- If you live in a widely-populated area, include a photo of a landmark near you, so the people can find you easily

- If you don't want your garage sale to start in the morning (and you should), then make sure your ad has the right time written on it

- Don't use cliché "Everything must go". It's a garage sale after all. It is obvious you are trying to sell everything, this just wastes space on your ad. Your mission is to make your ad stand out, you don't want to make it similar to someone else's.

- Even though you need to include the time when your garage sale starts, you are not obligated to include the closing time. Sometimes, the closing time just lets people know how desperate you are to sell you items, so they can use that fact as leverage against you in an effort to get a better deal.

- If you do include the closing time, be prepared for the last-minute bargain shoppers and competiton between buyers (in case they both want the same thing). If you don't have many items to sell, then a closing time might not be a bad idea, instead point out, it is a "limited time offer".

- To make your ad stand out, don't forget to mention any collectible or rare items you want to sell. This will attract more buyers.

- Your ads should be published at least one week before your garage sale. When it comes to online ads, you can choose to place it on local free websites like Craigslist.com, or Backpage.com. The day before your garage sale, don't forget to post a reminder.

- The same ad that is published on Craigslist.com, or in newspapers can be published on your social media profiles like Facebook, or Google+. This will attract even more potential buyers to your garage sale.

- If you are creating a community garage sale, with your neighbors, then include your ad in the local newspapers events section.

- NOTE: if you are organizing a multi-day garage sale, then treat it seperately, i.e. publish separate ads for each day. Why? Because if people see a multi-day ad they will assume if they arrive on the second day of your garage sale that all good stuff will be gone. Treating every day separately will bring in a bigger profit.

- When including photos in your ad on Craigslist.com, do NOT upload them directly to the website, because their clarity will decrease. Instead, choose some photohosting website like Flickr.com, or Photobucket.com and include the link to your Cragislist ad.

Tips for People in Rural Areas

If you live in a rural area, and you can't rely on traffic or a lot of people seeing your ad. In order to have successful garage sale, you should:

- Publish the ad one or two weeks before the garage sale

- Make sure you place your ads in nearby towns

- Advertise in newspapers

- Coordinate the date of your garage sale with a big event that takes place in your town.

- Place street signs in places with more traffic

- Include detailed instructions about the location
- Involve neighbors or family to get more visitors.

REMEMBER: if, for any reason, you change your mind or something happens and you're not able to have your garage sale, make sure you cancel the ads, or to use your social media accounts etc. to let everybody know there won't be garage sale. That is the responsible thing to do.

Garage Sale Flyers

The flyers that inform people about your garage sale should include:

- Listed items that will be included in the garage sale
- Photos
- Details about date, location, and time
- Tell people why they should visit your garage sale
- And also, never use "Everything must go"

Headlines That Will Attract More Attention

Naturally, the attention of readers and passers-by need to be grabbed with the headline. Some of the headlines that are good for garage sales include:

- HUGE RANGE OF ITEMS
- BIG CLEAN OUT
- BARGAIN HUNTER'S GARAGE SALE
- 10% OF SALES TO BE DONATE TO CHARITY (and make sure you do that)
- ANNUAL GARAGE SALE
- STUFF TO RESELL
- PERFECT STUFF FOR EBAY, BUT I AM TOO LAZY
- IF I WERE YOU, I WOULD BUY SOMETHING
- ONE DAY GARAGE SALE AT_____, ON_____

Additional Info

When publishing flyers, you should:

- Browse Google images to get some ideas

- Include tear-offs (little slips they can tear off the paper with the garage sale information)
- Place them on community boards and in shop windows
- Send flyers to second-hand shop owners
- Make your own signs (be creative)
- If you don't like doing arts and crafts, you can buy signs on sassysigns.com, and websites like Amazon, and Garage Sale Tools.

To sum it up, you can publish your ads on social media outlest, Craigslist, and local newspapers. Also, you can make all sorts of flyers to inform people about your garage sale. Be specific, include a lot of details, and don't use too many cliches.

Chapter 4: Rules and Tips For Successful Garage Sale

Garage sales aren't easy and require a lot of time. It is especially tough on people who are throwing their first garage sale. In order to make things easier, and to simplify the entire process, below are tips and rules to make your first garage sale profitable and successful.

Tips and Rules for profitable Garage Sale

- Collect enough stuff – before you decide to throw a garage sale, make sure you have enough stuff that you want to sell. This may sound too simple, but people often find it hard to get rid of something, or sell it, even though they have already decided they will include that specific item in their sale.

- Ask someone to help you – you will not be able to do it all by yourself. Garage sales require a lot of work, so asking your spouse, friends, or family to help is a good idea. Also, on the day of the sale you can ask your teenager to help.

- Move your car – your car should not be parked in front of your house. You should leave this parking space open to the potential buyer

- Sale items don't have to be from inside your house – you can include gardening tools, or plants in your garage sale.

- As already mentioned, give something for free in order to gain more profit.

- Visit different garage sales before throwing your own. See how they price and display items and conduct their sale.

- Make sure all merchandise you want to sell is nicely displayed. Don't just throw it out on your lawn and leave it there.

- Remember how to price your items – the prices shouldn't be too high, nor too low. And ask yourself if you would pay that much for the item.

- Make lemonade or ice tea and offer it to buyers.

- Be friendly, but also remain in the background – when a buyer arrives, say hello and be friendly. However, nobody likes a pushy seller, don't follow your customers around. Give them their own space to shope and time to think about whether they want something or don't.

- When choosing items for sale, make sure you include as much items as possible. You never know what someone is looking for, so offer a wide variety of products.

- The most interesting items should be closer to the curb to get a buyers' attention.

- You need to make sure you have enough change in the form of small bills and coins.

- Keep money in a safe place

- If the product you want to sell comes with the original box, keep it, and offer it to your buyer.

- Before the garage sale, come up with a plan of what are you going to do with the unsold products. You can decide to save them for another garage sale, or you can donate them.

- Before the garage sale, check to see if your city or town has a law that requires getting a permit for a garage sale. If so, get one.

- Arrange the tables, and place all merchandise carefully.

- Clothes should be on a hanger, or folded nicely.

- Make sure everything you sell (clothes, shoes, toys, furniture etc.) are clean. Nobody likes to buy dirty stuff.

- At least one hour before the garage sale starts, you should be outside, sorting everything, arranging signs etc.

- If you are throwing your garage sale during summer, bring a fan to make your buyers more comfortable in the heat.

- If you have helpers, make sure the person who's handling the money is good with the math (if you don't have time to do it yourself)

- Count the change back to your customer, and make sure they see how much money you are giving to them.

- Make sure you have a SOLD sign on furniture etc. that a person can't take home right away.

- Make sure you have a tape measure in case someone wants to purchase something but are not sure about the dimensions.

Safety Tips

While garage sales are practical, they attract a lot of people (even people you don't know), so you have to be careful and remember these tips:

- Never talk about how much money you are making
- Never let anyone in your house
- Lock all your doors
- Every helper you have needs to know what their role is.
- Don't ignore your customers, don't chit chat and ignore what your customers are doing
- If you have pets, keep them inside.
- When it comes to negotiating and bargain, don't do it right away. Start around noon, (you don't want to give everything away for less money than you wanted too early).

Preparing for Garage Sale

Your garage sale items need to be prepared, but you have to be ready also. Here are some ideas.

- Get enough sleep the night before

- Come up with a to-do list where you keep everything you need to do in the morning. The list will remind you in the event you forget to do something. Keeping a list is key for good organization and planning.

- Make sure everything is priced, unpacked, and ready

- Open your garage door according to the schedule

- Rearrange items from time to time to make tables look full after other merchandise has sold.

- When the sale is over, clean everything, remove all the signs, and pack everything carefully.

Garage sales require a lot of work, however with the help you can do it easily. Make sure everything is priced the right way, be polite, and include helpers with different tasks.

Your first garage sale can be profitable if you follow and pay attention to all the advice and tips we have offered in this book.

NOTE: If the closing time (or if it's afternoon and there is relatively not much traffic), and you still have a lot of stuff left – don't despair.

Just go around with your price tags, and lower their price. You can also come up with a new offer for the next buyer to ensure they will make a purchase. Everything can be done with a little bit of creativity, and your garage sale can be profitable and successful, but also it is great lesson for your next garage sale.

Chapter 5: Why are Garage Sales Profitable for Buyers Too

Garage sales aren't only good for sellers. They are good for buyers too. It can be said that garage sales are a win-win situation, where both sides close the deal happy and satisfied.

People visit garage sales for numerous reasons like:

- They like good deals

- They like to bargain

- They like socializing with other people from different neighborhoods

- People visit garage sales because they can find hidden treasures

- Garage sales are good sources of quality things for a lower price

- They need things for a collection

- They love to buy broken things and fix them

- They love to buy and sell various things to sell on eBay

- Some people actually buy stuff at garage sales and sell them for a living.

Most Popular Garage Sale Items

As it was already mentioned, garage sales are win-win situations. Here is a list of most-searched for items, and most popular items at garage sales to make even more profit:

- Old cellphones – teenagers love to buy them, and resell them on eBay.

- Baby clothes, shoes, and toys

- Magazines, or comic books – appreciated by collectors

- Wedding-related items

- Pregnancy clothes

- Power tools (saws, drills, etc.)

- Sports equipment

- Electronics

- Bicycles

- Household appliances (refrigerator, irons, dicers, juicers)

- Books

- Furniture

- Gardening equipment

- Jewelry (rings, watches, necklaces)

- Beddings

- Shoes, boots, and coats

- Linens, especially vintage.

Famous Garage Sale Purchases

- In the year 2000, Rick Norsigian purchased some glass plates for $45 at the Los Angeles warehouse salvage sale. Later, it was confirmed that the glass plates were actually original photographic negatives by the famous nature photographer Ansel Adams. The real worth of these negatives today is $200,000,000.

- In the year 2008, Tony Marohn bought a box which contained old papers at a garage sale for $5 and later discovered they were certificates for an oil company that was acquired by Coca Cola. Today they are worth – 130,000,000.

- In the year 2012, a man bought an art sketch for only $5. It was discovered later that sketch was actually Andy Warhol's original painting worth $2,000,000.

Ideally, you have lots of items that fit into more categories, and with the right ads, flyers, and pricing, you can make a significant profit.

If you offer nice services and reasonable prices, you can even ask buyers to leave their phone number so you can contact them when you decide to arrange your next garage sale. They will recommend you to others, and your items so the next event can be even more profitable.

Also, bear in mind that you need buyers as much as they need you. Without your buyers you wouldn't be able to get rid of all your stuff and to make a lot of profit (that is your goal after all). That is why you have to be patient, and polite.

Chapter 6: Garage Sale Fun Facts

In order to make garage sales even more interesting than they are, here are some fun facts that will inspire you to throw your own garage sale event.

- In the early 1800s, garage sales were different. Unclaimed cargo was sold in shipping yards at discounted price. The events were called "rommage sales".

- In the late 1800s rommage sales became rummage sales, and their location moved from the shipping docs to charity bazaars, or churches and other community spaces.

- Garage sales as we know them today, started in the 1950s or 1960s after World War II. As cities were expanding and people were looking for houses with garages and yards increased.

- Through the 1970s and 1990s garage sales become even more popular as the economy grew, people are constantly in demand for new products and merchandise. As a result, they want to sell or get rid of products they have owned before.

- In the 1990s and 2000's, people used the internet in order to find all the garage sales in their area. That is when garage sale ads become popular online, and in newspapers too.

- Now, there are even apps where people are able to find all garage sales in their area. Not only that, people are even able to find out what items they can find at certain locations. With the rise of internet, the popularity of good deals garage sales grew (that is why your ads have to be perfect which will guarantee the profit).

- The world's longest garage sale is The 127 Corridor Sale – held on National Garage Sale Day (already mentioned above; the second Saturday in August) and it spans 690 miles along Highway 127 from Michigan all the way to Alabama. Thousands of sellers participated in this event.

Garage Sale in Numbers

165,000 – the estimated number of garage sales every week in the United Sates.

690,000 – the estimated number of buyers who purchased something at garage sales every week.

4,967,500 – the estimated number of items and products that are sold at garage sales every week.

$4,222,375 – the estimated total US weekly revenue from garage sales.

$0.85 – the estimated average price of garage sale item.

Conclusion

Thank you again for downloading this book!

I hope this book helped you to learn more about garage sales, its purposes, rules and pricings. The goal of this book was to help you create and run your very own garage sale and earn killer profits.

The next step upon successful completion of this book is to start deciding what items should be at your garage sale, decide when to throw your event, and check if you need to acquire any permits. If not, go ahead and get rid of that old stuff that you don't use anymore and earn some money.

Throughout this book you now understand that garage sales require a lot of patience and dedication. Also, not only are they are helpful, they are one of the activities that has been a part of our culture for hundreds of years.

Now that you know how to plan, conduct, and price the items that will be included in your garage sale.

Go ahead, start your own garage sale and make some money.

Finally, if you enjoyed this book, please take the time to share your thoughts and post a review on Amazon. It'd be greatly appreciated!

Thank you and good luck!

Book # 5

Day Trading for Beginners

7 Steps to Earning $2,000 per Month Day Trading in Less than 20 Hours a Week!

Copyright © 2015

All rights are reserved. No part of this book may be reproduced in any form without permission in writing from the author. Reviewers may quote brief passages in reviews.

Disclaimer

No part of this publication may be reproduced or transmitted in any form or by any means, mechanical or electronic, including photocopying or recording, or by any information storage and retrieval system, or transmitted by email without permission in writing from the publisher.

While all attempts and efforts have been made to verify the information held within this publication, neither the author nor the publisher presumes any responsibility for errors, omissions or opposing interpretations of the content within.

This book is for entertainment purposes only. The views expressed are those of the author alone, and should not be taken as expert instruction or commands. The reader of this book is responsible for his or her own actions when it comes to reading the book.

Adherence to all applicable laws and regulations, including international, federal, state, and local governing professional licensing, business practices, advertising, and all other aspects of doing business in the US, Canada, or any other jurisdiction is the sole responsibility of the purchaser or reader.

Neither the author nor the publisher presumes any responsibility or liability whatever on the behalf of the purchaser or reader of these materials.

Any received slight of any individual or organization is purely unintentional.

Table of Contents

Introduction

Chapter 1 - Day Trading, what is it?

Chapter 2- Starting the journey of day trading

Chapter 3- Penny stocks rates fluctuations

Chapter 4- trade minimum position size

Chapter 5- trading for profitability

Chapter 6 -direct access broker

Conclusion

Introduction

My congratulations and appreciation for the download of the book, "Day Trading for Beginners - 7 Steps to earning $2,000 per Month Day Trading in Less than 20 Hours a Week!"

This book contains proven steps and strategies for "making $2,000 per month." I am sharing my life experience of day trading here. This book is a step by step guide of day trading. We will give you seven steps, not joking, seven steps that will help you learn the essential tips, tricks and perks of day trading.

If you take the time to read this book entirely and apply, the information held within this book will help you in making your life more comfortable. You can fulfill your little dreams that are still left unfulfilled. With additional $2,000, I hope much better can happen. I hope you know an adage, "Money makes the mare go".

My continued gratitude for the download of this book, it is with great hope that you will enjoy it!

Chapter 1 Step One

Day Trading, What is it?

In this chapter, you will learn:

- *An understanding of day trading*
- *My life journey*
- *Overview of day trading*

Before starting our journey of earning $2,000 each month from day trading, we must make the term "day trading" clear. There is a lot of confusion to people about the meaning of day trading. This term is no doubt confusing, but don't worry. We will teach you each and everything step by step. And make you an expert yourself.

The day trading is a form of dealing with shares or a slightly different form in which one deals with currency. Individuals continuously buy and sell shares via the internet. The time span, as the name mentions, is one day. Thus, over the course of 1 day a person gets benefited and profited by minor price fluctuations in the share price.

The main problem with the day trading is law. A passed law in the United States state that you must have $25,000 in your account in order to trade shares. Since we are bound to the law, we need this amount of money to start for day trading of stocks. The case of currency trading is different. The main benefit is we do not need $25,000 to start. We can start with much less investment. Forex is a term used for trading money. It can be written as FX.

Now my advice, do not jump into the stock market. Don't deal with penny stocks, until you read this eBook. This book is a full guideline on day trading, its perks and benefits. Now what are the steps of day trading? I will start this eBook with my story.

My house's financial condition was not up to the mark. We were not very rich. Poor was the simplest term in which we could define ourselves. But I had a motivation. I wanted to do something to make my life easy and comfortable and financially stable. I already heard that many people are earning money via the internet. But I had no idea of how to make money through the internet. To gain the knowledge I started searching the internet. The way I got and many other people were using was investing. They simply invest money in the stock market. To me it was a great idea. But first I did a comprehensive research on the topic.

I did research on different topics like warren buffet, holding, CANSLIM, blue chip, etc. I studied about these topics thoroughly to get a better understanding of them.

Another fact that I learned was investing money in the stock market for a long term gives you only 10% on average. If you invest $10,000 in a year, in much research, such as looking at the company's cash flow, balance sheets, technical analysis and competition, you will get the benefit of only $1000 which is not sufficient for us to fulfill our dreams. Like we spent all year for just $1000.

But honestly speaking that was a very slow method of earning money. I needed something faster than this.

So I read different books, like "rich dad, poor dad" and in that book, I learned a basic rule. A rule to give you financial freedom. The rule was, "let your money work for you". So I took this rule and started to search ways how can I make the money work for me.

Then I get the idea of working in day trading. Day trading of penny stocks is the best way to earn daily, as the name mentions "day" trading. Let me make you clear. Let's say that you are working for penny stocks, and you buy a stock EFGH, for example. The rate of the stock is 0.1 and after a day it became 1 dollar. So a profit of 0.5. Well, that's cool. By working each day, I have earned a ton of money just by buying stocks and selling them at a margin. And that is how I made my money start working for me.

Now another question that pops up in any sensible person is, "which stock should I buy, which stock would give more profit?" And that question is a difficult question. So I did research again. I searched the internet thoroughly and with my hard work I finally came to a point.

I will share that too in this book, it is not just a book, it is my experience, my life strategy and how I made myself earn 2,000 dollars per month by working just for 18 to 20 hours.

Now coming to the chapter 1, I give you the ***Overview of day trading of penny stocks"***.

During your first alight to the business, confusion is your only sentiment. The main reason for the confusion is the terminologies in this business. By reading this chapter, you will learn where to start from.

First, you must familiarize with the terms used in the stock market. For you, I will provide a complete sample of such words. But don't worry, I'll explain each of them too.

Penny Stocks:

Penny stocks are the stocks that trade on the OTCBB. Now what is OTCBB, it is over the counter bulletin board. The price range of penny stocks is between 0.0001 to $5.00.

Market Makers:

Market makers are the ones who regulate and the penny stocks on the OTCBB.

DD:

It is an abbreviation of due diligence. Due diligence is the research and knowledge you must have before buying any stock. It is very important in this business.

Bid:

It is the price which the market makers are giving you or willing to give you to buy your shares. Or the price of your shares.

Ask:

It's the opposite of bidding. It is the selling price of your shares. Or it is the price at which you can buy different shares from the stock market.

Day trading as I already mentioned is actually selling and buying of shares within a single day. Well sounds interesting, why would anyone do that? The answer is obvious, i.e. making money and earning much profit in a short time span.

Let me give you another example. You buy a penny stock let's say, "Dawn" that worth 0.8. Another thing is you buy 1000 stocks of "dawn" having value of $800. The stock rises to $1 per stock over the period of a day. Now you get a profit of $200 in a day. And what is the working time behind that? Just working for an hour or two.

Now you have seen a profit of $200 in a day, and that is 20% profit. As I already told you that investing long term only yields 10% annually. But by day trading you can earn 10%, 20% or even 30% each day. And only penny stocks show such a rapid growth.

Now what steps should you do daily to earn this 10%, simply come up with the stocks that you wanted to trade that day, pick a reasonable stock, buy the stock, and sell it when you reach your desired percentage. A daily repeat of these steps will in no time start to earn you $2000 a month.

Chapter 2 Step Two

Starting the Journey of Day Trading

In this chapter, you will learn:

1. **Tools necessary for day trading**
2. **Trade commissions and fees**
3. **Trading restrictions**

Like every food has some ingredients, and everything in this universe is "based" on something. Similarly, day trading also needs something. It needs some appliances to start from. These appliances include the basic thing, which is an advance computer. The computer must have an internet connection. Now the internet connection choice is also very critical, it must be DSL or wireless. A powerful software, with real data and regular updates. I suggest you to you Microcap Feed. A guideline or, in other words, a complete knowledge secured in this book. Now why these things are needed. Let me explain them too in this guide.

A reliable and a fast computer is the key to success. When it comes to facts, it is obvious that everyone is in a great hurry in this world. In this world of hurry and haste, you must not own an old fashioned computer. You don't want your computer to be stuck again and again. The situation means restarting it again and again. Hence, you need a reliable and fast computer to protect your money, shares, and investment. It does not mean that you start planning to buy a superconductor, but a nice computer compatible with all these features. I suggest you to buy a Pentium IV. It would work best; even I worked on it from the start.

Fast internet connection is also the same thing. It is needed to speed up you buying and selling of shares. DSL now a day is the best and cheap as well. Its speed is satisfactory, enough to get your sales executed on time. The DSL charges are $20 per month. I don't think of it as a useless investment.

Similarly, every penny stock day trader must have an application named as Microcap Feed. The tool for use is the best there is in this business; to deal with your penny stocks. Microcap Feed will be discussed in detail further in this book.

The guide I am writing will also be helpful for your trades. Kindly take a look at it and gain a thorough knowledge of it. It will help you a lot in your journey. It is with evidence that many penny stock shares are of a high number and, as a result, to look for a flat commission broker is advisable. The technique saves you money levied by many brokers over the per-share surcharge. For instance, an extra $.01 for $2 stock is what Trade King tacks with the additional standard commission of $4.95. A trade of $500 dollars of a stock share adds $5 to your trade. An inquiry on other fees, is thus necessary before making any additions to a decision. It will always be of great importance in noting the difference in penny stock definition among different brokers.

A good penny stock broker will always give an additional allowance to unlimited trade shares at no extra cost. It is only a few that add more charge for large orders. The sluggishness in the trading strategy is due to additional commission pay forced on customers by brokers. The number of penny stock shares is a limit to the daily order.

The platform of your penny broke trade will be that of an online broker, a platform similar to that of a standard stock. An eye should be on firms proposing requisitions for the trade of penny stocks through a broker or imposed limits on the type of trade executed with them. An example will be where a large number of brokerages do allow customer access to short penny stocks. Some stock value range, like $0.05-$0.01, is undervalued.

The parent company of OpinionXpress shares a significant number of its penny stock policies with it. The access of a customer to a selection of penny stocks is high and at a flat rate since they eradicate the need for any other additional fees. The only limitation from the brokerage to the customer is the restriction from short stocks as active traders keep the idea in mind. The recent idea hub of the brokerage comes with excitement of combined functionality of different site tools giving way to categorical search of trade ideas. The inclusion goes from earning and volatility to market sentiment. The all-in-one trade ticket gets the best rate among many online brokerages. The availability of the tools is on the parent website and desktop platforms to the surprise of the users' preference lying on the side of the user-friendly website. Most traders are with access to brokerage live support and phone on the limitation of working hours. The services offered to customers ranging from emails receives good reviews even though the only slag to the process is the response time from the emails.

The Charles Schwab definition of a penny stock is fairly broad such that a value that is under $5 is a fair qualification. The economic commission structure of the brokerage is slightly flexible and possess no charges for hidden trading fees. The short on security is an allowance for customers with margin accounts, a selection of a majority of penny stock strategies. The value of the brokerage is high, rating aside the penny stock strategies evident to them. The after-hours trade surcharges are of non-existence. The access to Street-smart Edge is for clients with three or more monthly access gain. When it comes to research, Schwab is unbeatable, widening the selection of in-house experts and third party reports.

Among the very active traders, Interactive Brokers is a favorite. The workstation of the trading platform is one of the highly rated in the market. The functionality of the penny stocks places no limits on the company. Customers place limits or market orders and can short the securities. The catches are a few though. The securities that are not eligible to DTC are not available to clients for trade security. The trading gets pricey as the passing of all exchange fees is by the firm.

For professionalism and active trading, Cobra trading is a great fit. Four different platforms are about access to the clients through direct access trading, as a premium feature with the penny stocks in a large selection. The brokerage is similar to interactive brokers, allowing short penny stocks from brokers with both limit and market orders. A discount of up to 20% off is available for orders exceeding 250,000 shares. The functionality payment is the only requirement of the customers. To add to the already hefty fee on the platform, an exchange fee from the firm imposes on the customers of the penny stock.

Chapter 3 Step Three & Four

Penny Stocks Rates Fluctuations

In this chapter, you will learn,

1. *How to cope with the risks of Penny Stocks Rates*

2. *Using effective strategies*

3. *Risk factors*

Now what is the reason, why penny stocks fluctuate in their rate? It is a simple and basic rule. A rule economist use; demand and supply. Demand and supply are the vehicle that controls rate fluctuation of the penny stocks.

If something is in great demand, then surely its price would be high. If something is in less demand, the rate will be low. Similarly, if the supply is high, the rate is low, and if the supply is low, the rate will be high. Pretty simple, isn't it?

Now all we have to do is to change the factors in our favor. Which things are favorable for us? They are high demand while keeping low supply.

What to do to make the demand high? You should not have to analyze thoroughly to buy and sell stocks. Just pick the road of demand curve, i.e. it doesn't matter when you buy a stock and when you sell it. If you bought it and within the next minute its rate is high, or in other words the demand is high just selling it. Similar is the case applied to supply line.

Update yourself continuously from the news. News provides the highs and the lows of the stock exchange. The best example, every day trader best know is GLIF. GLIF is a penny stock. Its price gave its sellers a profit margin of 1000%. That's huge. Like if the person invested $1000 on GLIF, he made $10,000, a profit of $9000. Who doesn't want this profit? Everyone is eager of searching such penny stocks. But it is an example from the past.

There are relatively few investors in penny stock trading shares at any given time, unlike large exchange companies. Thus, the gain on paper may pose a difficulty when turning it into a liquid asset. Regardless of the negatives, an investor may be lucky or savvy to skyrocket their shares in a single day. The returns are usually exponential to their realization and in very short periods of time. Your penny stock investment should have a limit on the budget capital for use. Being stuck with the shares for some period, or total loss should not brush one's shoulder but some level of preparedness. But when the reward alights, it is of substance.

Investors make large profits due to sizeable volumes of shares purchased by traders and in turn the monetary changes in the stock's value are at a disadvantage. Considerable amounts of stock trade by speculators speculate an output with minimum investment. The risk of trading, by using short-term strategies, is less when compared to long term trend that randomly shift. The popularity of penny stocks leads to an artificial increase in stock values due to their purchase in large quantities by inexperienced investors. The substantial rise in the prices per share leads to a higher sale in the same stocks. Any penny stock business needs a thorough research prior to any investment opportunity. Historical analysis on the stock investment is of grave importance in order to gage a promising investment.

The increase in profits and decrease in risk is due to consistent trading and invested time on researching the same business. Most of the stock value change predictions are in use due to this strategy. The pickup of top penny stocks requires very efficient strategies when it comes to their analysis. The small generation of the number of sales every month is of small scale operations of penny stocks by many enterprises. The collapse of such companies is more likely than the substantial profits generated by small businesses. The company in question should be in a geographical region with numerous customers, and the business development should be of high demand products and services. Any enterprise considered while in the selection of penny stocks should be able to provide shares of high volume.

Well known stocks are always on hold by investors before they can be in use in the maximization of the same profits. The situation often leads to the sale of a company's assets or its purchase by a larger corporation. Generally, the values of top penny stocks are more volatile than any other. Experienced traders often purchase them at a value that is always on a frequent rise and with a fall that is by a significant margin.

The characteristic not only increases the level of risk, but also removes the doubt of uncertainty as the stocks can only be on hold for a short period. The maximization of such short-term profits initializes when the purchase of the type of assets is in large quantities. The significant drop in the penny stock value leads to liquidation of shares from some major shareholders to a purchase of the same stocks at lower prices. The fluctuation value of assets and their monitoring to an average price peak are on purchase at that moment. The riskiest of all stock investments are penny stocks. The judgment of the price change should be on whether it is temporarily just a blip or the fundamental outlook change of the company. Price manipulation often subjects unregulated penny stocks. Be wary of scammers convincing investors towards the purchase of stock by dumping the one they own after an exposure to bidding up of prices in the process. An additional risk to investors would be poor bidding. If the financial report of firms lack adequacy, accuracy, and timely delivery, informed decisions by investors would be very difficult. Thus, the findings define the penny stock company as corporate shells and nothing more with neither product nor service.

A trade through a broker requires an invitation of the disclosure statement from the same broker to the SEC. Truthfulness and honesty are important to oneself when performing the calculation of accumulated risk. Information gathering on penny stocks can be challenging during the launch of a research on the matter. Careful reading is considerable after the acquisition of an annual report with careful note of the business tips and irregularities that are a constant encounter. Significance can be available on the insider trading by assessing trade records, stock notes, trading patterns, and price movement. In any trading business, it is always wise to come up with an exit strategy.

Chapter 4

Trade minimum position size

In this chapter, you will learn:

1 Making smart trading decisions

2 Rome wasn't built in one day

3 Education on smart trading

There is no logic in the reason as to why you should make a trade that exceeds the minimum position size. The trading career, you begin, should be more about consistency other than making a living through trading. Consistency should be your backbone because the maximization of profit during a single trade does not make you a profitable trader. For this reason, you should opt to take advantage of the minimum positions until you are consistent in the money making business. The only reason, for not trading single minimum position size, would be when making future deals, like the ES and NQ. Your system is only impossible to follow the minimum position size of 1 contract when using scaling in or out. The available solution would be to use the ETF, such as SPY or QQQ. The technique allows one to scale in and out while trading small positions. It is not fair to worry about the BIG $$$ while still handling the SMALL $$$. The projection of the value and size is timely and always pops up somewhere along the trading career.

Trading should not be a prescription on how to scam you with million dollar bills in just a single day. The new career entered should expect realistic goals. Consistency and profitability in the first two years are not a guarantee as you will need to learn the tricks offered on the table. Expectations lowered to reasonable heights are a guarantee of thirst and hunger in climbing the lane of success.

A point, to note, to most traders, is that the opening of brokerage accounts is not the only stepping stone to money success. No surgery performed by any doctor is without taking time to study the causes and implications of the cause. The stock market is no different.

KOSPI 200 analysis for future markets proves a great deal of significance in the day trading activity. Most day traders are an attraction from the market's ample liquidity to transaction costs that are extremely low to an attraction of more traders. The outperformance of foreign investors to individual investors benefits only the brokerage firms and institutions through collected commissions of domestic day traders. A huge profit from superior foreign day traders directs its losses to domestic individual investors as a zero-sum-game is the reflected transaction.

The ability, of analyzing price movements on the part of the individual investors, leads to profit from research and strategic trading from the future markets. The popularity of day trading gains more faces due to the computerized trading systems. People are often caught unaware in an automation of negative thoughts. The possession of a cognitive journal by traders makes them better observers of their habitual thinking. One of the best sampled solutions for the commencement of a cognitive journal by traders is its integration to a trading journal. Most traders are equipped with a copy of their trade journals, placing a note on the trading setups, profits/losses, exits, parameters for stops, trade sizes, and the entries. The strengths and weaknesses of trading are a review by such a journal with insights that help a trader. The relationship between the trading results and a trader's state of mind is by connecting the alphabetical letters towards the re-evaluation of the traditional trade journal.

The latter point gains significance in terms of importance. The identification of negative thoughts by people leads to a non-recognition of their thinking an integral part of the pattern of their problems. An incorporation of thoughts in their description by a trading journal through behaviors, feelings, and thoughts to the placement, management and exiting of time trades creates an allowance to traders for the review their identity and self-talk in relation to consequences. By the adoption of the self-observer's role in the identification of the negative consequences and its thoughts, the process of divorce between the self and schemas by the trader begins. The first step towards progress is when people state and know if they are actually thinking or just being a part of a skeleton thought running through their head. The interruption of a pattern is usually a baby step in creating a diversion from its strength.

The beginning work is in the therapy of cognition, the journal maintenance, to an allowance of traders towards the identification of their negating thoughts in occurrence and an observation towards their impacts of destruction. The proficiency of traders towards the interruption of their automated thoughts, however, leads to the turnaround of their thoughts. In my practice, the most favored technique when it comes to disputation is the conversational role play by an audience with a situation of a familiar background. Interestingly, people who are immersed in their negated thoughts tend to be very supportive, encouraging, and positive of their peers with a similar dilemma. The assistance of Cognitive therapy is not the solution-finder to all negative-thoughts related problems.

Daily monitoring towards processing of person's with the aid of a cognitive journal finds use in the target of specified thought patterns for assistance and change in traders' recognition of connection; trading problems and negative schemas. The feeling is of active traders towards the creation of time for self-work of futures and options, but without the clarity of targets towards change, the dilution of self-improvement efforts are an option. Research brings a suggestion towards a direct correlation being drawn between the completion of assignments in cognitive homework and the eventuality in the succession of cognitive therapy. The ideology is towards the development of new, more positive thoughts of pattern, and this can only gain an accomplishment through the means of repetition.

Indeed, it would be a venture for me to say that such a therapy has a high likelihood of successful unless the traders possess a daily commitment towards self-work. It is of great difficulty to the imagination of not learning longstanding patterns with such inconsistency of unlimited effort.

Chapter 5 Step Six

Trading for profitability

In this chapter, you will learn,

1. *When to trade real money*

2. *The cost of trading*

3. *How to downside emotions when trading with real money*

The use of a trading simulator is of grave importance as a substitute for real money when the efforts of trying to make a profit are void. The trading simulator should act as a coach in order to prepare one for real money trade. The simulator engages one to consistency in his/her preparedness to join the real money trade option. The move is never swift due to the downsides in emotions when it comes to trading with real money.

In the normalcy of any trading business, cost is of equal importance. The costs should not be as low as to inhibit the right tools of use. The cost, of saving money, is only viable when making smart decisions and using the right "charting package". The cost of brokers varies, and your trading style is better suited based on the intelligent decision-making techniques. You should always seek better service delivery at a manageable cost.

Research studies also, have come up with a finding about the challenges inflicted by negative thoughts and its pattern. The finding is most likely to incur success if its conduction is in a fashion that is emotionally charged. The simple steps to filling out a cognitive journal with negligence to the confrontation of one's schema are a futile proof of an exercise that is not intellectually driven. The key to most success is the recognition and understanding of your *emotions* without further emulation. Once you let the effect of perfectionism to be more of a shadowing threat than the outcome of your image, you will have the empowerment of change to your longstanding planned patterns. In the realm of such a spirit, I ask you to be your own home exercise. The instance your automation of target thoughts are for change, the taping of a cue card set on a wall next to your monitor should be an advancement. An automation of a negative thought on each card is written. Next to your every thought will be an estimation of the cost incurred as a result of the thinking pattern. Prior to an involvement in each trade, it will be much simpler to get a scan of the cue cards in order to nix the involved impulses to the domination of the traded thoughts. The consistency in the performance of such an exercise may lead to a gradual appraisal of you becoming your own therapist.

The distinction in the physical and emotional manifestations is an accomplishment of the negating thought patterns. To the earliest realization of such manifestation, it will be of use to engage the shifting of emotional gears by the discontinuity of prior activities to an engagement in an alternate activity. Giving an example, your break from the train station may lead to the performance of some physical exercises that might be vigorous in nature. By the interruption of the flow of negating thoughts and substituting yourself towards a separate state, your come back to the situation will be of a different mode.

Ultimately, when it comes to our experiences, we are our own heirs. As our age gaps increases, our development is for an increase in rich and complex schemas, aiding us towards the understanding of more life experiences. The categorization of the filing cabinet in our mentality is a reflection of encountered life events. The internalization of positive schemas by people about themselves is due to the feeling of love and security. The negation of a mental map is, therefore, by a person with the experience of violence and rejection.

Chapter 6 Step Seven

Direct access broker

In this chapter, you will learn,

1. *What is a direct access broker*

2. *How to directly access to market*

3. *What direct access offer*

A direct access broker is a bypass from traffic to the trade market after placing your order. Online brokers like Charles Schwab, TD Ameritrade, and E*TRADE access through the web interface is much slower than on the software interface. For this reason, the quality of execution should be a trader's greatest concern when short listing a broker before the actual payment of a commission. Direct access offers a performance of superior quality that is in the form of greater control, speedier executions, and price improvements in order routing.

The customs brokers together with the company of other expertise in trading and Customs continually supply an audit, verification services, and a compendium of compliance to the importers. By the establishment of a verification standard and a third party compliance, a commencement is towards the reliance of such a body of work. The most crucial areas of trade are a focus for limited available resources. The verification and validation of an individual's license has no current means through the importation of brokerage or public firms.

Staying updated on the issues of modern business approaches together with the update of federal regulations on the world class is one of the best practices. The establishment of the delivery means and the criteria is by the regulators. In addition, the employment of the curriculum is by both the government and the private sector. The establishment of some monitoring or recording the educational standards from its minimum is a requirement. The inclusion could be the periodic variation of self-reporting. The expectation is the evolution into a compliance multiplier forming a bridge with the customer resources with more efficiency return on a prevailing investment

Conclusion

Thank you for reading this book entitled **"Day Trading for Beginners: Seven Steps to Earning $2,000 per Month Day Trading in Less than 20 Hours a Week!"** This book will have walked you through all the basics that you need to know in order to get started, as well as provided you with some tips to improve your skills quickly.

As you will have read, day trading has a lot of advantages for beginners, but it can also be ideal for more advanced trading for someone who would love to earn $2,000 each month. However, don't expect to be a brilliant trader straight away. You'll need to be prepared to build up your stocks, starting with very simple stocks and slowly moving on to more complex ones.

Making money after a few offset of a term and successful trading has a typical bridge called time. If your lifespan in the game is prolonged, not only will you learn trading, but your expertise in the game will gain a significant bonus. With Stops, a trader can maintain his/her status in the competition. Stops assist a trader in decision-making and analysis in order to cope up with risks. Any single trade has two outcomes like tossing a coin, you either win or lose. To provide a limit to your loss, stops are the most secure prescription.

Finally, if you've enjoyed this book, I'd like to ask you a favor; would you be kind enough to leave a review of this book on Amazon? It would be greatly appreciated.

Thank you and good luck!

Book # 6

Fulfilment by Amazon

How to Earn $5,000 a Month or More Selling on Amazon

FBA!

Copyright © 2015

All rights reserved. No part of this book may be reproduced in any form without permission in writing from the author. Reviewers may quote brief passages in reviews.

Disclaimer

No part of this publication may be reproduced or transmitted in any form or by any means, mechanical or electronic, including photocopying or recording, or by any information storage and retrieval system, or transmitted by email without permission in writing from the publisher.

While all attempts and efforts have been made to verify the information held within this publication, neither the author nor the publisher assumes any responsibility for errors, omissions, or opposing interpretations of the content herein.

This book is for entertainment purposes only. The views expressed are those of the author alone, and should not be taken as expert instruction or commands. The reader of this book is responsible for his or her own actions when it comes to reading the book.

Adherence to all applicable laws and regulations, including international, federal, state, and local governing professional licensing, business practices, advertising, and all other aspects of doing business in the US, Canada, or any other jurisdiction is the sole responsibility of the purchaser or reader.

Neither the author nor the publisher assumes any responsibility or liability whatsoever on the behalf of the purchaser or reader of these materials.

Any received slight of any individual or organization is purely unintentional.

Table of Contents

Introduction

Chapter 1 - FBA: How does It Work?

Chapter 2- What Every FBA Newbie Sellers Must Know

Chapter 3- Sourcing Inventory: What to Sell?

Chapter 4- More Tips for Selling Effectively

Chapter 5- Pack Your Shipments to Amazon Correctly

Chapter 6 -Things to Avoid When Using FBA

Conclusion

Introduction

I want to thank you and congratulate you for downloading the book, **"Fulfillment by Amazon - How to Earn $10,000 a Month or More Selling on Amazon FBA!"**

This book contains proven steps and strategies for achieving success on selling online via FBA.

Nowadays, many people would want and try various online businesses. However, many also believe and have this preconceived notions that they have to learn plenty of things and try several times before they can actually succeed in this kind of venture.

Self-limiting thoughts such as knowing how to code, must be a social media expert or should be able to develop attractive web sites were all myths in terms of FBA. This book will help you understand more what FBA is and how you can achieve success without knowing difficult technical stuff! Some of us may already experience failure in many online side-hustles thus; we become less motivated and eager to try others. So let this book be your guide and be equipped with the right knowledge to earn real money through FBA!

If you take the time to read this book fully and apply the information held within this book will help you to become successful with your online business and make it big to Amazon!

Thanks again for downloading this book, I hope you enjoy it!

Chapter 1

FBA: How Does It Work?

I assume you already heard of Amazon. We can consider it as a huge marketplace with hundreds of thousands possible buyers and sellers. Hence, there is a program called FBA or Fulfilment by Amazon which also has the similar principles as eBay: someone has some stuff to sell and is looking for potential buyers. However, the FBA program does more than just looking for buyers for you.

How FBA Differs?

Unlike its counterparts, **FBA takes care all of the necessary issues that sellers are usually stuck with**- Amazon serves as your business fulfilment center wherein you can sell stuff and they will take care of uploading the details of the product, packing and shipping it to its buyer and even managing the customer service for you!

Likewise, the process is very easy making it more convenient for the sellers. First, you source the products you wanted to sell through thrift stores, retail stores or stuff around your house. List them on Amazon under your seller account. Usually, the product pictures and details are all set for you. Include the prices for each product. Next, ship the products one at a time to Amazon. Amazon will then finds buyers, pack them and delivers each item. After they collected the payments and deduct their charges and fees, they will send the money, twice every month.

Things You Need to Get Started

FBA offers huge benefits and convenience at the same time but before you get started in selling your products, there are **3 major things** you need to accomplish first.

Amazon Seller Account -together with the Professional Selling Program, a seller account is a must. The FBA service costs $39.99 monthly which is relatively painless. Although the individual program does not require ongoing monthly fee, it has higher per item charge so getting the pro account is more practical.

Amazon App- you can download it for free and have it install in your device or smart phone for easy access to your account. If you don't have a smart phone, you can use your laptop or computer in scanning the products. If you find FBA amazing, then you must really invest in a great smart phone or device.

The product to sell or budget for scouting- FBA is an ideal way to get rid of the unnecessary stuff and unwanted things around the house but if you prefer to sell other things, prepare your budget for scouting products whether in your local grocery stores or retail stores.

To sum it up, Fulfilment by Amazon is a selling program wherein Amazon takes in-charge and virtually handles all the essential areas of the selling aspects. From listing your products and gears to storing and packing it and to making it available for Prime shipping, the program indeed offers convenience and help. Like any other programs, FBA sure has caveats which we will discuss further so you can avoid them.

Chapter 2

What Every FBA Newbie Sellers Must Know

Technical advancements made it possible and easier for us to find creative ways of selling and earning income online. The opportunities are endless however, keep in mind that there are no shortcuts to success. Like any "normal" jobs, being a Fulfilment by Amazon seller also requires hard work, patience, knowledge and selling skills. Likewise, there are other essential things to consider if you want to make it big with FBA.

Start-up capital - like any other business, a capital to begin with is important in FBA. Moreover, think of it as replacing an income from a regular job you have now. Any decent amount will do as long as it is enough to cover for the supplies or items to sell and inventory. An inventory is very important or you will end up not really knowing how your business is going on and what doesn't work for you. Remember that it takes money to make money.

Do not rely heavily on Amazon's reports - keeping your own records and detailed inventory will be very helpful for you in the long run. It will aid you in determining the actual product revenue, the costs of the goods, how can time affect your sales and so on.

Make multipacks and bundles- selling items in bundles or multipacks is very beneficial in various ways- lesser competition compared when selling single items and maximizing the Amazon fees. Whilst this method takes time and other resources, it will definitely pay-off.

Avoid the temptation to race to bottom - you will eventually notice that there are various sellers selling the same product like yours. There will be time that you might think of selling your product to a lower prices to attract buyers. Avoid being tempted to drop the prices too often or you will end up spending more for fees and other Amazon charges than gaining profit.

Do not rush things - you don't actually need to quit your regular job immediately and jump into FBA. Take time to plan things, set your goals and most importantly, save enough money before you quit. Remember that selling on Amazon FBA requires time for any sellers to build up their income adequate enough to support their needs and of their families. Also, FBA can be relatively new to you so take time to learn the process as much as you can. Hence, it will allow you to build a successful and solid, profitable business.

Join forums and related online groups- it is highly recommended for new FBA sellers to join any forums and online support groups related with Amazon FBA selling. Not only you will be surrounded with business minded people, you will also get numerous tips, strategies, helpful information and learn from other people's experiences. Likewise, be a reader and a learner to enhance your skills.

Believe that you can - apparently, success will be easier to achieve if you will believe in yourself and in what you can do. Working at home as entrepreneur and being your own boss can be somewhat stressful, doubtful and questionable for others but when you are surrounded by families and friends, you will eventually keep on track and make it big to FBA. Moreover, it will be extremely helpful if you will focus on your interests, enhance your skills and determine your expertise.

Follow the rules – like any organization or affiliates, Amazon also has lots of specific rules and regulation to follow. They do not often change these rules unlike eBay so you can easily learn and understand them. If you are looking for a specific rule or policy in selling, access the Seller Central and find the help button. Here you can type the policy you are looking for about your Amazon activities.

It can be safe to say that most of us would be dreaming of working at the convenience of their own homes and be their self's boss. This thought is becoming more and more possible every day with the various advancements we are enjoying today. However, before we actually jump in to this idea and start working at home, we need to assess ourselves first and find out if we have the certain characteristics that entrepreneurs must possess. Nonetheless, Amazon FBA selling is not for everyone so be equipped with the right knowledge to become successful.

Chapter 3

Sourcing Inventory: What to Sell?

As a beginner, you might have this notion that looking for items to sell is exactly the same as sourcing inventory for Amazon FBA. The latter is more on selling the products you can usually see in a thrift store or a retail store rather than selling items at a yard sale. There are a myriad of products and items to sell on Amazon. Soon you will learn of it and be able to find profitable items everywhere.

And due to the abundance of products to sell, one must practice being wise on their buying decisions by educating themselves on the kind and type of products to buy. You can encounter various profitable products so it will help to know where you can do your product sourcing.

Start Shopping at Your Own Shelves

You can be amazed discovering profitable products on your shelves, at the attic, in the garage and in other places at your home. Moreover, it is always advisable for beginners to take a look at their homes first and source for products. This will help you learn how to actually source products and at the same time, get rid of the unwanted, unnecessary things and make a fortune out of it.

This is also the cheapest way to start with your inventory. Eventually, you will find unused things or items that you only used once or twice. Your old cassette tapes, VHS, pottery set, ceramic vase and other things you received as a gift can be someone else's need. The whole process of selling on Amazon FBA is possible in your own home. Nonetheless, this is the first step to fill that inventory.

Garage Sales and Thrift Shops

You don't have to break your budget especially if you are just starting. Making a trip to yard sales, thrift shops and book sales will help you find profitable, inexpensive inventory. Likewise if you have very limited money, sourcing products in these places will help you to gain a decent return on investment without going overboard. You can also find awesome items at thrift stores and most of these shops regularly put new inventory so you can always find "new" items for your own inventory.

However, many of the find at thrift shops are considered "long-tail" items. This means that you must wait for the right buyer to look for it. And because most of the items are slightly used or pre-loved items, you have to clean and remove the stickers and price tags attached to it.

Retail Arbitrage- this is said to be the most popular among the strategies. You can source items in various retail stores to resell through FBA. Pharmacies, grocery stores, big box stores and toy stores are the most common places to source great product. Look for discounts, end caps and items on clearance that can bring you a nice return on investment. Moreover, you can also find items at a regular price that Amazon sells on a higher price.

Considering the law of supply and demand, stores and manufacturers will lower down the price of their products if they have large supply of it but are not moving. Eventually, there will be someone who is looking for that item across the country and will find yours on Amazon FBA. However, going after the same products like other sellers do will increase the competition. Replenishing the products can also be difficult.

Bulk Buying and Wholesaling - most sellers also love the idea of buying items in bulk and sourcing products in whole. There are various wholesale stores nowadays making it easier for FBA sellers to find items in bulk and have it multipack or sell in bundles without any competition.

The good thing is you can start with a minimum order like half dozen to "test" the demand of the product. It is also easier for these items to re-order especially if they sell very well. Likewise, you can build a good relationship with the manufacturer and wholesale suppliers and can have the exclusive rights to sell the items on Amazon. However, wholesale products may not also be too profitable since some of the wholesale distributors and sources can be hard to find. Most of them might not sell to Amazon FBA sellers due to competition.

The FBA program by Amazon is really an awesome online side hustle where you can literally work for a few hours only and be able to earn $10,000 or more every month! However, there are a number of ways and sourcing methods you have to learn and to determine if suitable for you. Moreover, the sales ranking of the products you will sell matters. You will learn more on this as we proceed.

Tons of sellers will say that a specific strategy works best such as retail arbitrage while others would say that wholesale resources are the best to choose. Nonetheless, so many options can be chosen from but keep in mind that these sourcing strategies will only work if one knows the work around first.

Chapter 4

More Tips for Selling Effectively

The business of buying and selling online requires big commitment from the sellers' part. Moreover, it requires capital and there are a lot of other things to consider. Also, you may not easily recover your return on investment in time to pay the necessary bills. Somewhat stressful, risky and challenging it is, being an online seller can be quite demanding for you.

Fortunately, the FBA program can help you in so many ways. They will sell the items on your behalf and manage customer interactions, packing and delivering the products for you. Less work is requiring from you in exchange of their handling fees and seller fees. Whilst Amazon itself will be a great help for you to sell, as a seller you also need to know how to sell effectively. Below are some of the proven selling tips that can help you.

Best sellers list - is where you can see high selling items in Amazon. There's a small link of "Best Sellers" per category where you can see products that are easy moving. Try to sell similar or items belong to this category.

Good reviews- selling items with good reviews is also an ideal strategy. You already have an idea what buyers are looking for in a product and what pleases them in terms of service and quality of goods.

New items- before buying products make sure first that Amazon will allow you to list it as new (assuming that it is). There are brands that doesn't allow this so do your research first and check if a certain item's condition has "new" in the drop down box in Amazon's page.

Competitive pricing- when we say price competitively, it doesn't require you to be too much competitive. When selling a popular product, simply match the price that Amazon's free shipping qualifies. If you decided to undercut the price, a penny or a dollar will do. Do not reduce the price too much or it will cause price war among other sellers with the same products.

Create unique items- utilize Amazon's Bundling Policy in creating unique items. Think of unique ways and come up with a unique product bundle if other sellers have the same item like yours. Making this strategy will increase your chance of winning the buy box. This is the page that comes up whenever a buyer clicks on the results upon searching Amazon. As per Amazon, almost 78% of the entire sales are from the buy box so winning it very crucial. However, there is a rule that when the bundle you created includes a media item such as a CD, you can list it under the media category. Moreover, you cannot combine a media item with other media products.

Describe the items clearly and accurately- while you may think this is a no brainer, most sellers tend to overlook this important part. To avoid negative feedbacks and returns, describe your products accurately in your listing. Customers mostly rely on descriptions upon purchasing items.

Customers Matter

- Amazon wants their sellers to answer their customer's queries within 24 hours or else, it will be a demerit to the seller's account. At the left page you can find the Seller Central where you can see customer's questions. On your account, you can also set the option of forwarding these questions to your email so you can answer it anytime.

- Customers or buyers in Amazon seldom leave feedback unless they were asked to. There are third party service providers where they will send your buyers automatic email stating how they can contact you if there are problems, questions and if there's something wrong with the products. It will help you prevent negative feedback situations to happen again.

- Work hard to remove negative feedbacks! Whenever you encounter a customer with negative things to say about you and your products, immediately reach out by sending him or her email with a sincere apology. Other sellers even include Amazon gift cards as token for their unsatisfied customers. However, do not abruptly ask the customer to remove the negative feedback rather, explain thru email what went wrong and assure them it won't happen again. Get over of the bad feedbacks as possible as you can to stay ahead of the game. To become **Amazon's feature seller**, you must consistently obtain 95% feedback rating or else, you will lose the chance and your account will be at stake.

Save Money While Selling

-Sell products with lower referral fees such as electronics, computers, cameras and unlocked cell phones. Other departments are more expensive compared to these.

- if you are planning to sell 40 or more products in a month, signing up for a Pro Merchant account is highly advisable. Amazon charges 99 cents as a fixed closing fee per item sold. The Pro Merchant will only cause you $39.99 a month and you can still downgrade to their free service anytime.

- You will encounter some customers who will return the product as damaged even if it is in good condition just so that they take advantage of the return for free policy. If this is the case, request the product to be returned to you and have it re-sell if it is still in good condition.

-Get advantage of the **JIT Inventory (Just in time)** to reduce your storage fees. This refers to getting your inventory just before it runs out. It will help you minimize the time your products are in the storage while having lesser cash tied-up in the inventory.

-Set an alert to determine the fast selling items in your inventory. The **Replenishment Alerts** by Amazon is a feature wherein you can set the alert at your preferred number of units and when an item reached that specific limit, Amazon will notify you through email. Likewise, this feature is very helpful for your ordering threshold and to avoid the delay of replenishing your items.

No High Risks and Heavy Items

It is not ideal to sell items through FBA that worth $50 or more. Most buyers think that they are actually buying their products to Amazon itself and not from third-party sellers. Hence, most of these buyers tend to make up stories, cheat, steal and scam towards this huge online-selling place. Refunds are very common and customers will tell you the outrageous reasons why you need to refund their money. Fragile items and expensive ones are not worthy to sell in FBA so make sure that you are only selling "easier" items to avoid problems with unnecessary refunds.

As much as possible, avoid selling heavy items as these are more expensive to ship to FBA warehouses due to tons of fees. Likewise, they are riskier in transits. Large but not oversized items are the best types to send in FBA as these items meet just the right threshold of weight and shipping fees.

As per **Amazon's guidelines**, the oversize rate will apply to any package that the longest sides reach 18" and weighs more than 20 pounds. Likewise, if the median side is more than 14" and the shortest sides are more than 8", the item will be considered oversized. It will cost you another $6 per oversize items so apparently, it is not worthy to sell them over FBA.

Sales Rank Matters

Selling items on FBA is more than just sourcing products you think would click in the market and shipping them off to Amazon's warehouse. You also need to consider the item's sales ranking. Selling items that are 3 million and beyond in rankings will only cost you more fees- storage fees, shipping fees and fees to have it removed because it is not selling. Likewise, disposing these items also cost money. If you are eager and willing to learn more, you will soon find out the essence of storage fees versus shipping fees versus sales ranking and how these affects your success in FBA selling.

Chapter 5

Pack Your Shipments to Amazon Correctly

Since Amazon will handle the storing and shipping of your products, you must pack and send your items to them properly. They are imposing fairly strict guidelines when sending items and products to the FBA warehouses. Likewise, you must abide there guidelines to avoid delays, damages and other penalty fees. Below are some of their rules in shipping.

Box size – choose the right box size for the items or units. Too large containers with insufficient items inside tend to collapse when placed under heavier boxes of same size of course, during the shipping process. It is advisable to use new, corrugated boxes with crust-strength stamp but you can also reused boxes from past shipments but make sure you have removed all the shipping labels to prevent confusion.

Wrapping and bundling - when wrapping, do not use paper over-wrap or string. Wrap the items separately. Only use strong tape specifically designed for shipping. You cannot bundle the boxes together by using elastic straps, bagging, extra straps or taping them. For bundles items, use poly bag as required by Amazon.

***Expiration dates*-** if sending treats, pet foods or any food items, make sure to include an expiration date label on the product and on the outside of the shipping box. It should be 6 months out upon sending to Amazon. Moreover, Amazon will destroy unsold, dated food products.

***Suffocation label*-** a poly bag with at least 5 inches or larger opening requires suffocation label. If the product arrives at Amazon without the suffocation label or product label, or requires them to do special handling before storing, a 75¢ handling fee per item will be charge to you. Likewise, you will receive warning notice for violating the said policy.

Labeling and Packing Requirements

Once or twice, we tend to easily mislabeled products especially when packing. New FBA seller can feel overwhelm while packing their box of items and shipping them off to Amazon's warehouse. There are specific rules on how to pack everything. Make sure to study and understand them to avoid committing errors and paying charges, losing items, damaging your products prior to shipping and gaining negative feedbacks from customers.

Customer Experience is the Ultimate Goal! Like any other business, Amazon's goal is to provide its customers one of a kind experience to win their loyalty and trust. Hence, every step is vital to deliver the customers the thrill along with their products. Quality is the key from how their items are boxed to how it was shipped at their doorsteps.

Find the perfect fit. When packing your items, make sure that the bag is tight-fitting without floppy corners. Too big poly bags can be used as handle for picking the items. You wouldn't like your product being tossed around with the possibility of tearing the bag.

Secure it. Always seal the poly bag with your items in it or the items will easily come off. Likewise, it can get lost easier especially if the FBA sticker is on the bag and not on the item. For boxes, fold the ends up and tape it. For fragile items, use a snug box or use small bubble wrap but do not overwrap.

Compact bundling helps. Do not bundle items as if they are cactus in a box. Make sure that the box is durable enough and try to put the items in a way that they won't flop around when the box is picked up. Remember that your items don't need to be aesthetically arranged when shipping it to Amazon instead, they have to be secured.

The FBA Label and bar code is very important. This is your product's link to you so make sure it properly attached to the box and to your product. Avoid putting it where it can be easily creased such as around corners of the box. Also, make sure that it contains a clean and readable bar code. Place it where it can be easily found. Thin bar codes along the label's edge can be damage easily so keep it centered. Moreover, hard to read bar codes can cause you problems during the process of shipping.

Manage the UPC's. If you intend to block the UPC with the FBA sticker, make sure to completely cover it and the UPC is unreadable. Putting a blank label in it is highly advisable since most scanners tend to read the first code that gets near their sensor. This is when problems arise, when the wrong bar code gets read.

Other Requirements

- When shipping t-shirts, packed them tightly to prevent them from winding up in a wad. Doing a military roll is highly advisable.

- Items made of hard plastics should be bagged appropriately to avoid it from mars and scuffs.

- Ensure that items with lids are also in tacked.

- Items with cloth, vinyl and leather surfaces can easily get dirty. Use poly bag for cloth and vinyl items and box the leather ones.

- Toys can be shrink-wrap or boxed.

- Do not use markers on any of your products.

- For eligible items, consider signing up for Amazon's Stickerless Commingled Inventory. This eliminates the need to label your eligible product separately (which means another fee). But if you want to, you can use the FBA Label Service so Amazon will label your eligible items for you.

The better an item is packed, the better chance of avoiding shipping problems. Always secure your items and ensure that it won't rattle inside its packaging. Likewise, avoid floppy corners and make each box scanner-friendly. Moreover, FBA works best if you are sending multiples of the same products. It is ideal to case packed your items in a box. This would be very beneficial as well because you don't have to send more items each time it sells out. Your customers can also order in multiples.

Remember, Amazon is a huge company and they tend to become rough on items delivered to them. We are talking about tons of items in boxes, cases and bags so they need to move as quickly as possible. Lastly, always do final checking before shipping your items. Create a check-list to ensure that things are in proper condition and the shipment will be smooth.

Chapter 6

Things to Avoid When Using FBA

Now that you already know the things you must do when selling through FBA, you should also learn the things to avoid. In a nutshell, the FBA service allows its sellers to store their product in their fulfillment centers. Every time you make a sale, they will handle the shipping, handling and even the customer service for you.

Hence, FBA will aid you to grow your sales by allowing you to focus more on other important matters aside from order fulfillment. To make the most out of the service and see maximum results, here are the common mistakes you cannot afford to make.

NOT UPDATING THE PRICE – changing your merchant-fulfilled listings to FBA means you also have to update the item's pricing. In merchant-fulfilled listings, the shipping credit and list price is included while in FBA, the list price is only required since shipping is free. However, the list price must be higher compared to the original merchant-fulfilled listing.

For an instance, you are selling an item worth $2.50 using merchant-fulfilled listing. You specified the shipping to cost $2.00. When you change to FBA listing without updating the price, the original shipping cost won't reflect as well as Amazon's listing commissions. You can easily make a mistake especially if you are new to FBA but you can do double-checking as well to prevent losing money.

CONFUSING DISTRIBUTED INVENTORY PLACEMENT AND COMINGLED SERVICES – these are two different ways of Amazon's labeling of inventory from individual sellers and from its own stocks. Look at it this way; the ***inventory placement service*** of Amazon allows seller to ship their standard-sized items to a single warehouse. The oversized items (as discussed earlier) will proceed to another warehouse. The seller has the option to pay a fee per product based on weight. The Amazon will further distribute the items to other warehouse which is their default option for sellers. This is called the *Distributed inventory placement* wherein you personally ship to other warehouses and since it is you, the seller, who handles this movement in this option, you are required to exert more time and effort but you will not pay a fee for each item.

On the other hand, the **Comingled inventory** is another option allowing the seller to store their products along with other similar products from other sellers and from Amazon. For example, you are selling a laptop case of a certain characteristics, size and manufacturer; it will be stored together with other items having the same descriptions. Amazon will then decide and draw from this collection of laptop case to fulfill orders. Apparently this is the least expensive among the choices but then again, you don't have any control over the quality and condition of the products your buyers will receive. It is up to you to decide if it is the fee or the fulfillment and the feedback that matters most.

Being careless on quality control- there will be instances that you are rushing things to obtain more sales hence, you tend to skimp on examining your products. Problems such as poor quality, missing products and wrong items delivered usually rise when a seller just rely on the barcode scanner and does not thoroughly verify the boxes' contents before sending them. Not only will your buyers lose faith in you and your service but Amazon too.

One can make the most of FBA Service by utilizing all its helpful features efficiently while maintaining their own store. While others think of this program too good to be true many would still consider taking their luck in Amazon FBA.

And since you are selling your items on Amazon's platform, there's no need for you to do some marketing and advertising your online business. Nonetheless, your success in Amazon FBA depends on how much you would want to learn and familiarize yourself with ins and outs of the entire process.

Conclusion

Thank you again for downloading this book!

I hope this book was able to help you to deeply understand how Amazon FBA Service works and what is in store for you!

The next step is to apply all the knowledge, selling tips and other advice written in this book.

Start small, slowly but surely. I wouldn't suggest you to quit your regular job now but consider all the advantages and of course, the huge earnings that you can have with FBA. Business-minded persons that don't have the necessary equipment and space for their inventories are fortunate that Amazon has FBA service. You too can get advantage of this service and start making $10,000 or more in a month!

From teapots, to apparels, to power tools and software, FBA can be the perfect partner in distributing your items and making your small business a success. Furthermore, Amazon offers world-class fulfillment that will help you grow your sales and earn loyal customers.

Finally, if you enjoyed this book, please take the time to share your thoughts and post a review on Amazon. It'd be greatly appreciated!

Thank you and good luck!

www.ingramcontent.com/pod-product-compliance
Lightning Source LLC
Chambersburg PA
CBHW020743180526
45163CB00001B/335